General Explanations
of the
Administration's Fiscal Year 2011
Revenue Proposals

Department of the Treasury
February 2010

TABLE OF CONTENTS[1]

---

[1] The Administration's primary policy proposals reflect changes from a tax baseline that modifies current law by "patching" the alternative minimum tax, freezing the estate tax at 2009 levels, and making permanent a number of the tax cuts enacted in 2001 and 2003. The baseline changes to current law are described in the Appendix. In some cases, the policy descriptions in the body of this report make note of the baseline (e.g., descriptions of upper-income tax provisions), but elsewhere the baseline is implicit.

TEMPORARY RECOVERY MEASURES

EXTEND THE MAKING WORK PAY CREDIT

Current Law

The Making Work Pay (MWP) credit is a temporary provision of the American Recovery and Reinvestment Act of 2009 (ARRA). In 2010 individual taxpayers are eligible for a refundable income tax credit equal to 6.2 percent of earned income up to a maximum credit of $400 ($800 for married taxpayers filing a joint return). Thus, workers receive a credit on the first $6,452 of earned income ($12,903 for married taxpayers filing a joint return). The credit is phased out by 2 percent of a taxpayer's modified adjusted gross income (AGI) in excess of $75,000 ($150,000 for married taxpayers filing a joint return). Dependent filers are not eligible for the credit.

In 2009, adults who received social security benefits, railroad retirement benefits, veterans benefits, pension benefits from a Federal, state or local government or Supplemental Security Income (SSI) benefits (excluding individuals who receive SSI while in a Medicaid institution) received either an Economic Recovery Payment of $250 or a special tax credit of $250 ($500 in case for a married couple filing jointly where both spouses are eligible). Individuals who were entitled to both the MWP credit and either the $250 Economic Recovery Payment or the special tax credit for 2009 were required to reduce the amount of their MWP credit, but not below zero, by the amount of their Economic Recovery Payment or special tax credit.

The IRS withholding schedules have been modified to reflect the MWP credit. Overwithholding and underwithholding are reconciled on annual income tax returns.

The MWP credit expires at the end of 2010.

Reasons for Change

The MWP credit partially offsets the regressivity of the Social Security payroll tax. It effectively raises the after-tax income of workers eligible for the credit, which makes work more remunerative and so encourages individuals to enter the labor force. Furthermore, the ability of many taxpayers to receive the credit through reduced withholding, rather than after the end of the tax year, increases the incentive effects of the credit. Extending the credit would allow the positive benefits of the credit to continue during the period in which the economy is still recovering from the recession.

Proposal

The proposal would extend the MWP credit for one year through December 31, 2011.

PROVIDE $250 ECONOMIC RECOVERY PAYMENTS AND SPECIAL TAX CREDIT

Current Law

The American Recovery and Reinvestment Act of 2009 (ARRA) provides a refundable tax credit based on earned income. For 2009 and 2010, the Making Work Pay (MWP) credit is equal to 6.2 percent of earned income, up to a maximum credit of $400 ($800 for married taxpayers filing a joint return). The credit is phased out at a rate of 2 percent of a taxpayer's modified adjusted gross income (AGI) in excess of $75,000 ($150,000 for married taxpayers filing a joint return). Dependent filers are not eligible for the credit.

ARRA also provided a one-time $250 payment for certain retirees and a $250 refundable tax credit for recipients of government pensions who were not eligible for the $250 payments.

Economic Recovery Payments: A $250 Economic Recovery Payment was made in 2009 to each adult who was eligible ($500 to a married couple filing jointly where both spouses were eligible) for Social Security benefits, Railroad Retirement benefits, veterans benefits, or Supplemental Security Income (SSI) benefits (excluding individuals who receive SSI while in a Medicaid institution). Only individuals eligible to receive at least one of these benefits in the three-month period prior to February 2009 were eligible for an Economic Recovery Payment. Individuals received only one Economic Recovery Payment even if they were eligible for more than one type of benefit.

Special Tax Credit for Certain Government Retirees: Federal, State and local government retirees who received a pension or annuity from work not covered by Social Security and who were not eligible to receive an Economic Recovery Payment were entitled to claim a $250 refundable income tax credit ($500 for a married couple filing jointly where both spouses are eligible) for 2009.

Individuals who were entitled to both the MWP credit and either the $250 Economic Recovery Payment or the special tax credit for 2009 were required to reduce the amount of their MWP credit, but not below zero, by the amount of their Economic Recovery Payment or special tax credit.

Reasons for Change

The Economic Recovery Payments and special tax credit are intended to provide economic assistance to retirees similar to the assistance provided to workers through the MWP credit. During the period in which the economy is still recovering, it is appropriate to continue to provide similar benefits for retirees.

Proposal

The Administration proposes to provide a $250 Economic Recovery Payment in 2010 to each adult who is eligible ($500 to a married couple filing jointly where both spouses are eligible) for Social Security benefits, Railroad Retirement benefits, veterans benefits, or Supplemental Security Income (SSI) benefits (excluding individuals who receive SSI while in a Medicaid institution). The Administration also proposes to provide a $250 refundable tax credit in 2010 to Federal, State, and local government retirees who are not eligible for Social Security benefits and who are not eligible to receive an Economic Recovery Payment ($500 for a married couple filing jointly where both spouses are eligible for the credit). Retirees who are employed and eligible for the MWP credit would have their MWP credit reduced (but not below zero) by the amount of the Economic Recovery Payment or refundable tax credit.

EXTEND COBRA HEALTH INSURANCE PREMIUM ASSISTANCE

Current Law

COBRA[1] requires certain employers (generally private-sector and State and local government employers with 20 or more employees) and certain other entities that maintain group health plans to offer certain individuals ("qualified beneficiaries") the opportunity to elect to continue coverage under the group health plan for a specified period after the occurrence of certain events such as termination of employment, that otherwise would have caused a termination of coverage. To obtain COBRA continuation coverage, qualified beneficiaries generally must pay a premium, which generally cannot exceed 102 percent of the cost of similar coverage for active employees. A group health plan that fails to comply with the COBRA continuation coverage rules is subject to an excise tax.

Under a separate provision of the law, Federal employees and their families are also entitled to temporary continuation coverage under the Federal Employee Health Benefit Program (FEHBP) if coverage ends as the result of termination of employment. In addition, many States have laws or regulations that provide continuation coverage in the case of a loss of group health plan coverage; these rules often apply in the case of a loss of coverage under a group health plan maintained by a small employer not subject to Federal COBRA continuation coverage requirements.

The American Recovery and Reinvestment Act of 2009 ("ARRA") in certain circumstances limits the employee's cost of purchasing continuation coverage to 35 percent of the COBRA premium charged by the group health plan. The ARRA COBRA premium assistance may also apply to temporary continuation coverage elected under FEHBP and to State programs that provide coverage comparable to COBRA. Employers (or other entities providing the coverage) are allowed a credit against payroll taxes for the remaining 65 percent of the premium. Under ARRA, as amended,[2] the premium assistance is available for a maximum of 15 months (ending sooner if a qualified beneficiary becomes eligible for coverage under another group health plan or Medicare or if the period of COBRA continuation coverage otherwise ends). The premium assistance is limited to qualified individuals who qualify for COBRA coverage as a result of an involuntary termination of employment between September 1, 2008 and February 28, 2010. The premium assistance is recaptured for individuals with modified adjusted gross income above $145,000 ($290,000 for married taxpayers filing jointly), with the recapture phased in for individuals with modified gross income above $125,000 ($250,000 for married taxpayers filing jointly).

ARRA included special transition and notice rules allowing certain individuals who lost coverage on account of an involuntary termination of employment prior to enactment of the

---

[1] "COBRA" is the acronym for the law that added the continuation coverage rules to the Code, the Consolidated Omnibus Budget Reconciliation Act of 1985.

[2] The premium assistance provisions were amended on December 19, 2009, by the Department of Defense Appropriations Act, 2010 (DOD Act) to extend the duration of the premium assistance from 12 months to 15 months and to extend from December 31, 2009 through February 28, 2010, the period during which involuntary terminations of employment will qualify for assistance.

4

premium assistance additional opportunities to elect premium assistance with respect to COBRA continuation coverage.[3]

Reasons for Change

As the economic recovery continues, it is appropriate to extend COBRA premium assistance to help individuals who lose their employer-provided health coverage when they lose their jobs.

Proposal

The proposal would extend the COBRA premium assistance eligibility period by allowing qualified individuals who qualify for COBRA coverage as the result of an involuntary termination of employment prior to January 1, 2011 to qualify for the assistance. The duration of the COBRA premium assistance that results from an involuntary termination of employment after February 28, 2010 would be 12 months.

Appropriate transition relief would be provided to ensure that COBRA premium assistance is available for individuals who become qualified as a result of an involuntary termination of employment after February 28, 2010, and before enactment of the extension (if not enacted before March 2010).

---

[3] Special transition relief was also provided as part of the extension enacted by the DOD Act.

PROVIDE ADDITIONAL TAX CREDITS FOR INVESTMENT IN QUALIFIED PROPERTY USED IN A QUALIFYING ADVANCED ENERGY MANUFACTURING PROJECT

Current Law

A 30-percent tax credit is provided for investments in eligible property used in a qualifying advanced energy project. A qualifying advanced energy project is a project that re-equips, expands, or establishes a manufacturing facility for the production of: (1) property designed to produce energy from renewable resources; (2) fuel cells, microturbines, or an energy storage system for use with electric or hybrid-electric vehicles; (3) electric grids to support the transmission, including storage, of intermittent sources of renewable energy; (4) property designed to capture and sequester carbon dioxide emissions; (5) property designed to refine or blend renewable fuels or to produce energy conservation technologies; (6) electric drive motor vehicles that qualify for tax credits or components designed for use with such vehicles; and (7) other advanced energy property designed to reduce greenhouse gas emissions.

Eligible property is property: (1) that is necessary for the production of the property listed above; (2) that is tangible personal property or other tangible property (not including a building and its structural components) that is used as an integral part of a qualifying facility; and (3) with respect to which depreciation (or amortization in lieu of depreciation) is allowable.

Total credits are limited to $2.3 billion, and the Treasury Department, in consultation with the Department of Energy, was required to establish a program to consider and award certifications for qualified investments eligible for credits within 180 days of the date of enactment of the American Recovery and Reinvestment Act of 2009. Credits may be allocated only to projects where there is a reasonable expectation of commercial viability. In addition, consideration must be given to which projects: (1) will provide the greatest domestic job creation; (2) will have the greatest net impact in avoiding or reducing air pollutants or greenhouse gas emissions; (3) have the greatest potential for technological innovation and commercial deployment; (4) have the lowest levelized cost of generated or stored energy, or of measured reduction in energy consumption or greenhouse gas emission; and (5) have the shortest completion time. Guidance under current law requires taxpayers to apply for the credit with respect to their entire qualified investment in a project.

Applications for certification under the program may be made only during the two-year period beginning on the date the program is established. An applicant that is allocated credits must provide evidence that the requirements of the certification have been met within one year of the date of acceptance of the application and must place the property in service within three years from the date of the issuance of the certification.

Reasons for Change

The $2.3 billion cap on the credit has resulted in the funding of less than one-third of the technically acceptable applications that have been received. Instead of turning down worthy applicants who are willing to invest private resources to build and equip factories that manufacture clean energy products in America, the program should be expanded. An additional

$5 billion in credits would support at least $15 billion in total capital investment, creating tens of thousands of new construction and manufacturing jobs. Because there is already an existing pipeline of worthy projects and substantial interest in this area, the additional credit can be deployed quickly to create jobs and support economic activity.

Proposal

The proposal would authorize an additional $5 billion of credits for investments in eligible property used in a qualifying advanced energy project. The guidance that requires taxpayers to apply for the credit with respect to their entire qualified investment will be modified so that taxpayers can apply for a credit with respect to only part of their qualified investment. If a taxpayer applies for a credit with respect to only part of the qualified investment in the project, the taxpayer's increased cost sharing and the project's reduced revenue cost to the government will be taken into account in determining whether to allocate credits to the project.

Applications for the additional credits would be made during the two-year period beginning on the date on which the additional authorization is enacted. As under current law, applicants that are allocated the additional credits must provide evidence that the requirements of the certification have been met within one year of the date of acceptance of the application and must place the property in service within three years from the date of the issuance of the certification.

The change would be effective on the date of enactment.

EXTEND TEMPORARY INCREASE IN EXPENSING FOR SMALL BUSINESS

Current Law

Section 179 of the Internal Revenue Code provides that, in place of capitalization and subsequent depreciation, taxpayers may elect to deduct a limited amount of the cost of qualifying property placed in service each taxable year, subject to a phase-out that begins at a specified level of qualifying investment. For qualifying property placed in service in taxable years beginning in 2007 and in 2010, the maximum deduction amount is $125,000. For these years, the maximum deduction is reduced (but not below zero) by the amount by which the cost of qualifying property exceeds $500,000. Both the limit and the phase-out level in 2010 are indexed for inflation after 2006. For taxable years 2008 and 2009, the maximum deduction is $250,000 and the phase-out begins at $800,000. For qualifying property placed in service after 2010, the limits revert to pre-2003 law, with $25,000 as the maximum deduction and $200,000 as the beginning of the phase-out, with no indexing for inflation. Higher expensing amounts are allowed for qualified disaster assistance property and investments in an empowerment zone or renewal community.

In general, qualifying property is defined as depreciable tangible personal property and certain depreciable real property that is purchased for use in the active conduct of a trade or business. For taxable years beginning after 2002 and before 2011, off-the-shelf computer software is considered qualifying property even though it is intangible property.

Reasons for Change

Section 179 benefits many small business taxpayers and the economy. Expensing encourages investment by reducing the after-tax cost of capital purchases, relative to claiming regular depreciation deductions. Expensing is also simpler than claiming regular depreciation deductions, which is particularly helpful for small businesses. Extending to 2010 the limits in effect for 2008 and 2009 would encourage investment and promote economic recovery.

Proposal

The Administration's tax receipts baseline assumes that the rules under section 179 that are in effect for 2010 will be extended permanently, so that there will be a maximum deduction of $125,000 and a phase-out threshold of $500,000, indexed for inflation after 2006.

The proposal would extend to qualifying property placed in service in a taxable year beginning in 2010 the rules under section 179 that are in effect for taxable years beginning in 2008 and 2009. The maximum amount of qualifying property that a taxpayer may deduct would be $250,000 and the phase-out would begin at $800,000 of qualifying investment. Qualifying property would include off-the-shelf computer software.

EXTEND TEMPORARY BONUS DEPRECIATION FOR CERTAIN PROPERTY
Current Law

An additional first-year depreciation deduction is allowed for qualified property placed in service during 2008 and 2009. The deduction equals 50 percent of the cost of qualified property placed in service, and is allowed for both regular tax and alternative minimum tax purposes. The property's depreciable basis is adjusted to reflect this additional deduction. However, the taxpayer may elect out of additional first-year depreciation for any class of property for any taxable year.

Qualified property for this purpose includes tangible property with a recovery period of 20 years or less, water utility property, certain computer software, and qualified leasehold improvement property. Qualified property must be new property. Qualified property excludes property that is required to be depreciated under the alternative depreciation system (ADS), as well as qualified New York Liberty Zone leasehold improvement property. The taxpayer must purchase (or begin the manufacture or construction of) the property after December 31, 2007 and before January 1, 2010 (but only if no written binding contract for the acquisition was in effect before January 1, 2008). The property must be placed in service before January 1, 2010. An extension by one year of the placed in service date is allowed for certain property with a recovery period of ten years or longer and certain transportation property, if the property has an estimated production period exceeding one year and a cost exceeding $1 million. Only the portion of the basis that is properly attributable to costs incurred prior to January 1, 2010, may be taken into account. Certain aircraft not used in providing transportation services are also granted a one-year extension of the placed-in-service deadline. Special rules apply to syndications, sale-leasebacks, and transfers to related parties of qualified property.

Corporations otherwise eligible for additional first-year depreciation may elect to claim additional research or minimum tax credits in lieu of claiming the additional depreciation for "eligible qualified property." Such property only includes otherwise qualified property that was acquired after March 31, 2008, and only basis attributable to the property's manufacture or construction after that date is taken into account. Depreciation for such property must be computed using the straight-line method.

Reasons for Change

By accelerating in time the recovery of investment costs, the additional first-year deduction for new investment lowers the after-tax costs of capital purchases. This encourages new investment and promotes economic recovery.

Proposal

The proposal would extend the additional first-year depreciation deduction for one year, generally for property acquired and placed in service during 2010 (or placed in service during 2011 for property eligible for a one-year extension of the placed-in-service date). The election for claiming additional research or minimum tax credits in lieu of the additional depreciation deduction would also be extended by one year. Corporations would be allowed to choose whether or not to make an election with respect to qualified property placed in service in 2010, regardless of prior-year elections of the provision. The proposal would be effective for qualified property placed in service after December 31, 2009.

EXTEND OPTION FOR CASH ASSISTANCE TO STATES IN LIEU OF LOW-INCOME HOUSING TAX CREDITS

Current Law

In general, section 42 of the Internal Revenue Code provides an income tax credit (the low-income housing tax credit, or LIHTC) equal to the applicable percentage of qualified basis in a newly constructed or substantially rehabilitated qualified low-income residential rental property (determined based on residency by tenants with incomes below prescribed levels). The applicable percentage is adjusted monthly by the IRS, with reference to the Applicable Federal Rate, such that over ten annual installments the credit will have a present value of, in the case of Federally subsidized housing, 70, or otherwise 30, percent of qualified basis (with enhancement in qualified census tracts and difficult development areas). However, pursuant to the Housing Act of 2008, the applicable percentage for non-Federally subsidized new buildings placed in service before 2014 shall be not less than 9 percent. The aggregate credit amount that may be allocated within a State may not exceed a credit ceiling based on population, and State housing agencies allocate credit amounts, pursuant to a qualified allocation plan, among qualified low-income buildings, which the State housing agencies physically inspect. Under the Housing Act of 2008, qualified basis shall not include any building costs financed with the proceeds of a Federally-funded grant. Qualified basis may be reduced with respect to certain financing not considered to be at-risk. Noncompliance with certain section 42 requirements may result in recapture of a portion of the credit, with interest.

The American Recovery and Reinvestment Act of 2009 (ARRA) allows State housing agencies to elect to receive a cash amount (as determined under the ARRA) in lieu of a portion of the State's 2009 LIHTC credit ceiling. State housing agencies must use the cash to make subawards to finance the acquisition or construction of qualified low-income buildings, generally subject to the same requirements (including rent, income, and use restrictions on such buildings) as the LIHTC allocations. The State housing agency is required to perform asset management functions to ensure compliance with the LIHTC rules and the long-term viability of buildings financed with subawards. In case of noncompliance, the State housing agency is to determine whether recapture of the subaward is warranted and, if so, to collect the recapture amount and effectuate repayment to the Treasury. Although taxpayer privacy law generally would apply to return information collected by the Treasury in connection with tax liability, cash assistance information is not confidential return information as so defined.

Reasons for Change

The ARRA makes cash assistance available for low-income housing even in situations in which tax credits may be of limited utility to investors. Extending the provision would allow cash assistance to continue to be available for low-income housing. Under the ARRA, the State housing agency supervises compliance of a cash subawardee; meanwhile, the IRS is responsible for monitoring compliance with the parallel section 42 provisions. Because cash subawards and credits may be claimed with respects to the same qualified low-income buildings, it may be more efficient for the IRS to have jurisdiction over cash subawardee compliance as well.

Proposal

The proposal would allow States to elect cash assistance in lieu of low-income housing tax credits for 2010. The cash assistance for each State could not exceed an amount equal to 85 percent of the product of ten and the sum of the State's: (1) unused housing credit ceiling for 2009; (2) returns to the State during 2010 of credit allocations (other than credit allocations derived, directly or indirectly, under section 1400N(c) of the Code) made by the State in a prior year; (3) 40 percent of the State's 2010 per capita authority: and (4) 40 percent of the State's share of the 2010 national pool allocation, if any. States would be required to use the cash assistance by December 31, 2012, to finance the construction or rehabilitation (including acquisition) of qualified low-income housing projects generally subject to the same rental requirements and recapture rules as properties financed with LIHTC.

A Federal agency other than the IRS would continue to administer elections by State housing agencies to receive cash in lieu of a portion of the State's LIHTC allocation. State housing agencies would continue to inspect qualified low-income buildings that received a cash subaward, but would report noncompliance to the IRS. The IRS would be authorized to determine whether recapture of the subaward is warranted and, if so, to collect the recapture amount. If a State housing agency has a lien or regulatory agreement secured by a qualified low-income building, the agency would assign the lien or agreement to the IRS for collection by Federal authorities. Although taxpayer privacy law generally would apply to information gathered by the IRS for collection purposes, the amount of a subaward for a qualified low-income building would not constitute confidential return information, as under current law. The IRS would be authorized to audit a subawardee under administrative provisions parallel to those applicable to taxpayers claiming the LIHTC, including recourse to the IRS Office of Appeals. Judicial review of a compliance action would be authorized to parallel that for a corresponding LIHTC action (e.g., a subawardee may seek to avoid recapture in Tax Court, after exhausting administrative remedies, or may seek to recover a recapture amount in District Court).

TAX CUTS FOR FAMILIES AND INDIVIDUALS

EXPAND THE EARNED INCOME TAX CREDIT (EITC)

Current Law

Low and moderate-income workers may be eligible for a refundable earned income tax credit (EITC). Eligibility for the EITC is based on the presence and number of qualifying children in the worker's household, adjusted gross income (AGI), earned income, investment income, filing status, age, and immigration and work status in the United States. The amount of the EITC is based on the presence and number of qualifying children in the worker's household, AGI, earned income, and filing status.

The EITC has a phase-in range (where each additional dollar of earned income results in a larger credit), a maximum range (where additional dollars of earned income or AGI have no effect on the size of the credit), and a phase-out range (where each additional dollar of the larger of earned income or AGI results in a smaller total credit). The EITC for childless workers is much smaller and phases out at a lower income level than does the EITC for workers with qualifying children.

The EITC generally phases in at a faster rate for workers with more qualifying children, resulting in a larger maximum credit and a longer phase-out range. In 2010, the credit reaches its maximum at three qualifying children. This provision expires after 2010, at which point workers with three or more qualifying children will receive the same EITC as similarly situated workers with two qualifying children.

The phase-out range for joint filers begins at a higher income level than for an individual with the same number of qualifying children who files as a single filer or as a head of household. The width of the phase-in range and the beginning of the phase-out range are indexed for inflation. Hence, the maximum amount of the credit and the end of the phase-out range are effectively indexed.

The following chart summarizes the EITC parameters for 2010.

	Childless Taxpayers	Taxpayers with Qualifying Children		
		One Child	Two Children	Three or More
Phase-in rate	7.65%	34.00%	40.00%	45.00%
Minimum earnings for maximum credit	$5,980	$8,970	$12,590	$12,590
Maximum credit	$457	$3,050	$5,036	$5,666
Phase-out rate	7.65%	15.98%	21.06%	21.06%
Phase-out begins	$7,480 ($12,490 joint)	$16,450 ($21,460 joint)	$16,450 ($21,460 joint)	$16,450 ($21,460 joint)
Phase-out ends	$13,460 ($18,470 joint)	$35,535 ($40,545 joint)	$40,363 ($45,373 joint)	$43,352 ($48,362 joint)

To be eligible for the EITC, workers must have no more than $3,100 of investment income. (This amount is indexed for inflation.)

Reasons for Change

Families with more children face larger expenses related to raising their children than families with few children and as a result tend to have higher poverty rates. The steeper phase-in rate and larger maximum credit for workers with three or more qualifying children helps workers with larger families meet their expenses while maintaining work incentives.

Proposal

The proposal would make permanent the expansion of the EITC for workers with three or more qualifying children. Specifically, the phase-in rate of the EITC for workers with three or more qualifying children under the American Recovery and Reinvestment Act of 2009 (ARRA) would be maintained at 45 percent, resulting in a higher maximum credit amount and longer phase-out range.

The proposal would be effective for taxable years beginning after December 31, 2010.

EXPAND THE CHILD AND DEPENDENT CARE TAX CREDIT

Current Law

In 2010, taxpayers with child or dependent care expenses who are working or looking for work are eligible for a nonrefundable tax credit that partially offsets these expenses. Married couples are eligible only if they file a joint return and either both spouses are working or looking for work, or if one spouse is working or looking for work and the other is attending school full-time. To qualify for this benefit, the child and dependent care expenses must be for either (1) a child under age thirteen when the care was provided or (2) a disabled dependent of any age with the same place of abode as the taxpayer. Any allowable credit is reduced by the aggregate amount excluded from income under a dependent care assistance program.

Eligible taxpayers may claim the credit for up to 35 percent of up to $3,000 in eligible expenses for one child or dependent and up to $6,000 in eligible expenses for more than one child or dependent. The percentage of expenses for which a credit may be taken decreases by 1 percentage point for every $2,000 (or part thereof) of AGI over $15,000 until the percentage of expenses reaches 20 percent (at incomes above $43,000). There are no further income limits. The phase-out point and the amount of expenses eligible for the credit are not indexed for inflation.

Reasons for Change

Access to affordable child care is a barrier to employment or further schooling for some individuals. Assistance to individuals with child and dependent care expenses increases the ability of individuals to participate in the labor force or in education programs.

Proposal

Under the proposal, the AGI level at which the credit begins to phase out would be permanently increased from $15,000 to $85,000. The percentage of expenses for which a credit may be taken would decrease at a rate of 1 percentage point for every $2,000 (or part thereof) of AGI over $85,000 until the percentage reached 20 percent (at incomes above $113,000). As under current law, there would be no further income limits and the phase-out point and the amount of expenses eligible for the credit would not be indexed for inflation.

The proposal would be effective for taxable years beginning after December 31, 2010.

PROVIDE FOR AUTOMATIC ENROLLMENT IN IRAS AND DOUBLE THE TAX CREDIT FOR SMALL EMPLOYER PLAN STARTUP COSTS

Current Law

A number of tax-preferred, employer-sponsored retirement savings programs exist under current law. These include section 401(k) cash or deferred arrangements, section 403(b) programs for public schools and charitable organizations, section 457 plans for governments and nonprofit organizations, and simplified employee pensions (SEPs) and SIMPLE plans for small employers.

Small employers (those with no more than one hundred employees) that adopt a new qualified retirement, SEP or SIMPLE plan are entitled to a temporary business tax credit equal to 50 percent of the employer's plan "startup costs," which are the expenses of establishing or administering the plan, including expenses of retirement-related employee education with respect to the plan. The credit is limited to a maximum of $500 per year for three years.

Individuals who do not have access to an employer-sponsored retirement savings arrangement may be eligible to make smaller tax-favored contributions to individual retirement accounts or individual retirement annuities (IRAs).

IRA contributions are limited to $5,000 a year (plus $1,000 for those age fifty or older). Section 401(k) plans permit contributions (employee plus employer contributions) of up to $49,000 a year (of which $16,500 can be pre-tax employee contributions) plus $5,500 of additional pre-tax employee contributions for those age fifty or older.

Reasons for Change

For many years, until the recent economic downturn, the personal saving rate in the United States has been exceedingly low, and tens of millions of U.S. households have not placed themselves on a path to become financially prepared for retirement. In addition, the proportion of U.S. workers participating in employer-sponsored plans has remained stagnant for decades at no more than about half the total work force, notwithstanding repeated private- and public-sector efforts to expand coverage. Among employees eligible to participate in an employer-sponsored retirement savings plan such as a 401(k) plan, participation rates typically have ranged from two-thirds to three-quarters of eligible employees, but making saving easier by making it automatic has been shown to be remarkably effective at boosting participation.

Beginning in 1998, Treasury and the IRS issued a series of rulings and other guidance (most recently in September 2009) defining, permitting, and encouraging automatic enrollment in 401(k) and other plans (enrolling employees by default unless they opt out). Automatic enrollment was further facilitated by the Pension Protection Act of 2006. In 401(k) plans, automatic enrollment has tended to increase participation rates to more than nine out of ten eligible employees. In contrast, for workers who lack access to a retirement plan at their workplace and are eligible to engage in tax-favored retirement saving by taking the initiative and making the decisions required to establish and contribute to an IRA, the IRA participation rate tends to be less than one out of ten.

Numerous employers, especially those with smaller or lower-wage work forces, have been reluctant to adopt a retirement plan for their employees, in part out of concern about their ability to afford the cost of making employer contributions or the per-capita cost of complying with tax-qualification and ERISA (Employee Retirement Income Security Act) requirements. These employers could help their employees save -- without employer contributions or plan qualification or ERISA compliance -- simply by making their payroll systems available as a conduit for regularly transmitting employee contributions to an employee's IRA. Such "payroll deduction IRAs" could build on the success of workplace-based payroll-deduction saving by using the excess capacity to promote saving that is inherent in employer payroll systems, and the effort to help employees save would be especially effective if automatic enrollment were used. However, despite efforts more than a decade ago by the Department of the Treasury, the IRS, and the Department of Labor to approve and promote the option of payroll deduction IRAs, few employers have adopted them or even are aware that this option exists.

Accordingly, requiring employers that do not sponsor any retirement plan (and that are above a certain size) to make their payroll systems available to employees and automatically enroll them in IRAs could achieve a major breakthrough in retirement savings coverage. In addition, such a requirement may lead many employers to take the next step and adopt an employer plan (permitting much greater tax-favored employee contributions than an IRA, plus the option of employer contributions). The potential for the use of automatic IRAs to lead to the adoption of 401(k)s, SIMPLEs, and other employer plans would be enhanced by raising the existing small employer tax credit for the startup costs of adopting a new retirement plan to an amount significantly higher than both its current level and the level of the proposed new automatic IRA tax credit for employers.

In addition, the process of saving and choosing investments in automatic IRAs could be simplified for employees, and costs minimized, through a standard default investment as well as electronic information and fund transfers. Workplace retirement savings arrangements made accessible to most workers also could be used as a platform to provide and promote retirement distributions over the worker's lifetime.

Proposal

Employers in business for at least two years that have more than ten employees would be required to offer an automatic IRA option to employees, under which regular contributions would be made to an IRA on a payroll-deduction basis. If the employer sponsored a qualified retirement plan, SEP, or SIMPLE for its employees, it would not be required to provide an automatic IRA option for its employees. Thus, for example, a qualified plan sponsor would not have to offer automatic IRAs to employees it excludes from qualified plan eligibility because they are covered by a collective bargaining agreement, under age eighteen, nonresident aliens, or have not completed the plan's eligibility waiting period. However, if the qualified plan excluded from eligibility a portion of the employer's work force or a class of employees such as all employees of a subsidiary or division, the employer would be required to offer the automatic IRA option to those excluded employees.

The employer offering automatic IRAs would give employees a standard notice and election form informing them of the automatic IRA option and allowing them to elect to participate or opt

17

out. Any employee who did not provide a written participation election would be enrolled at a default rate of three percent of the employee's compensation in an IRA. Employees could opt out or opt for a lower or higher contribution rate up to the IRA dollar limits. Employees could choose either a traditional IRA or a Roth IRA (with Roth being the default). For most employees, the payroll deductions would be made by direct deposit similar to the direct deposit of employees' paychecks to their accounts at financial institutions.

Payroll-deduction contributions from all participating employees could be transferred, at the employer's option, to a single private-sector IRA trustee or custodian designated by the employer. Alternatively, the employer, if it preferred, could allow each participating employee to designate the IRA provider for that employee's contributions or could designate that all contributions would be forwarded to a savings vehicle specified by statute or regulation.

Employers making payroll deduction IRAs available would not have to choose or arrange default investments. Instead, a low-cost, standard type of default investment and a handful of standard, low-cost investment alternatives would be prescribed by statute or regulation. In addition, this approach would involve no employer contributions, no employer compliance with qualified plan requirements, and no employer liability or responsibility for determining employee eligibility to make tax-favored IRA contributions or for opening IRAs for employees. A national web site would provide information and basic educational material regarding saving and investing for retirement, including IRA eligibility, but, as under current law, individuals (not employers) would bear ultimate responsibility for determining their IRA eligibility.

Contributions by employees to automatic IRAs would qualify for the saver's credit (to the extent the contributor and the contributions otherwise qualified), and the proposed expanded saver's credit could be deposited to the IRA to which the eligible individual contributed.

Employers could claim a temporary tax credit for making automatic payroll-deposit IRAs available to employees. The amount of the credit for a year would be $25 per enrolled employee up to $250, and the credit would be available for two years. The credit would be available both to employers required to offer automatic IRAs and employers not required to do so (for example, because they have not more than ten employees).

In conjunction with the automatic IRA proposal, to encourage employers not currently sponsoring a qualified retirement plan, SEP, or SIMPLE to do so, the "startup costs" tax credit for a small employer that adopts a new qualified retirement, SEP, or SIMPLE plan would be doubled from the current maximum of $500 per year for three years to a maximum of $1,000 per year for three years. This expanded "startup costs" credit for small employers, like the current "startup costs" credit, would not apply to automatic or other payroll deduction IRAs. The expanded credit would be designed to encourage small employers that would otherwise adopt an automatic IRA to adopt instead a new 401(k), SIMPLE, or other employer plan instead, while also encouraging other small employers to adopt a new employer plan.

The proposal would become effective January 1, 2012.

EXPAND SAVER'S CREDIT

Current Law

A nonrefundable tax credit is available for eligible individuals who make voluntary contributions to 401(k) plans and other retirement plans, including IRAs. The maximum annual contribution eligible for the credit is $2,000 for single taxpayers or married individuals filing separately. In the case of a married couple filing jointly, the maximum annual contribution eligible for the credit is $2,000 for each spouse (for a total of up to $4,000). The resulting maximum credits are $1,000 and $2,000, respectively. The credit rate is 10 percent, 20 percent or 50 percent, depending on the taxpayer's adjusted gross income (AGI). The AGI thresholds for the credit are subject to adjustment each calendar year based on increases in the cost-of-living. In 2010, "eligible individuals" who may claim the credit are

Married couples filing jointly with incomes up to $55,500,

Heads of households with incomes up to $41,625, and

Married individuals filing separately and single taxpayers with incomes up to $27,750, who are eighteen or older, other than individuals who are full-time students or claimed as a dependent on another taxpayer's return.

The credit is available with respect to an eligible individual's "qualified retirement savings contributions." These include: (i) elective deferrals to a section 401(k) plan, section 403(b) plan, section 457 plan, SIMPLE, or simplified employee pension (SEP); (ii) contributions to a traditional or Roth IRA; and (iii) other voluntary employee contributions to a qualified retirement plan, including voluntary after-tax contributions and voluntary contributions to a defined benefit pension plan. The eligible individual may direct that the amount of any refund attributable to the credit be directly deposited by the IRS into an IRA or certain other accounts.

The credit is nonrefundable and, therefore, only offsets regular tax liability or alternative minimum tax liability. The credit is in addition to any deduction or exclusion that would otherwise apply with respect to the contribution.

Reasons for Change

The saver's credit should be amended to more effectively encourage moderate- and lower-income individuals to save for retirement. Because it is currently nonrefundable, the saver's credit only offsets a taxpayer's income tax liability and therefore offers no saving incentive to tens of millions of households without income tax liability. In addition, to provide a stronger incentive, the credit rate should be increased for most eligible households, the current three-tier credit rate structure should be simplified, and the number of eligible households should be increased by raising the income thresholds. Finally, making the saver's credit more like a matching contribution would enhance the likelihood that the credit would be saved and would increase the salience of the incentive by framing it as a match similar to the familiar employer matching contributions to 401(k) plans.

19

Proposal

The proposal would offer a more meaningful saving incentive to tens of millions of additional households by making the saver's credit fully refundable and raising the eligibility income threshold to cover millions of additional moderate-income taxpayers. The proposal also would raise the credit rate and simplify the current three-tier credit structure by prescribing a uniform 50 percent credit rate, and would allow the credit to be deposited automatically in the qualified retirement plan account or IRA to which the eligible individual contributed.

In place of the current 10-percent/20-percent/50-percent credit for up to $2,000 of qualified retirement savings contributions per individual, the proposal would provide a 50-percent refundable credit that effectively matches 50 percent of the first $500 of such contributions per individual (allowing a married couple filing a joint return to make up to $1,000 of such contributions) per year, indexed annually for inflation beginning in taxable year 2012). Accordingly, the maximum credit would be $250 for a single filer and $500 for a married couple filing a joint return.

The eligibility income threshold would be increased to $65,000 for married couples filing jointly, $48,750 for heads of households, and $32,500 for single taxpayers and married individuals filing separately, with the amount of contributions eligible for the credit phased out at a 5-percent rate for AGI exceeding those levels (so that some amount of credit would be available to joint filers with AGI between $65,000 and $85,000).

The proposal would be effective for taxable years beginning after December 31, 2010.

EXTEND AMERICAN OPPORTUNITY TAX CREDIT

Current Law

Prior to enactment of the American Recovery and Reinvestment Act of 2009 (ARRA) an individual taxpayer could claim a nonrefundable Hope Scholarship credit for 100 percent of the first $1,200 and 50 percent of the next $1,200 in qualified tuition and related expenses (for a maximum credit of $1,800) per student. The Hope Scholarship credit was available only for the first two years of postsecondary education.

Alternatively, a taxpayer could claim a nonrefundable Lifetime Learning Credit (LLC) for 20 percent of up to $10,000 in qualified tuition and related expenses (for a maximum credit of $2,000) per taxpayer. Both the Hope Scholarship credit and LLC were phased out in 2009 between $50,000 and $60,000 of adjusted gross income ($100,000 and $120,000 if married filing jointly). In addition, through 2009, a taxpayer could claim an above-the-line deduction for qualified tuition and related expenses. The maximum amount of the deduction was $4,000.

ARRA created the American Opportunity Tax Credit (AOTC) to replace the Hope Scholarship credit for taxable years 2009 and 2010. The AOTC is partially refundable, has a higher maximum credit amount, is available for the first four years of postsecondary education, and has higher income phase-out limits.

The AOTC equals 100 percent of the first $2,000, plus 25 percent of the next $2,000, of qualified tuition and related expenses (for a maximum credit of $2,500). Under ARRA, the definition of related expenses for both the LLC and the AOTC was expanded to include course materials. Forty percent of the otherwise allowable AOTC is refundable (for a maximum refundable credit of $1,000). The credit is available for the first four years of postsecondary education. The credit phases out for taxpayers with adjusted gross income between $80,000 and $90,000 ($160,000 and $180,000 if married filing jointly).

All other aspects of the Hope Scholarship credit are retained under the AOTC. These include the requirement that AOTC recipients be enrolled at least half-time.

Reasons for Change

The AOTC makes college more affordable for millions of middle-income families and for the first time makes college tax incentives partially refundable. If college is not made more affordable, our nation runs the risk of losing a whole generation of potential and productivity.

Making the AOTC partially refundable increases the likelihood that low-income families will send their children to college. Under prior law, low-income families (those without sufficient income tax liability) could not benefit from the Hope Scholarship credit or the Lifetime Learning Credit because they were not refundable. Under the proposal, low-income families could benefit from the refundable portion of the AOTC. In combination with Federal Pell grants, these grants and refundable credits would cover all tuition and fees at an average two-year public college and about half of tuition and fees at an average four-year public college.

Moreover, the AOTC is available for the first four years of college, instead of only the first two years of college, increasing the likelihood that students will stay in school and attain their degrees. More years of schooling translates into higher future incomes (on average) for students and a more educated workforce for the country.

Finally, the higher phase-out thresholds under the AOTC give targeted tax relief to an even greater number of middle-income families facing the high costs of college.

Proposal

The proposal would make the AOTC a permanent replacement for the Hope Scholarship credit. To preserve the value of the AOTC, the proposal would index the $2,000 tuition and expense amounts, as well as the phase-out thresholds, for inflation.

This proposal would be effective for taxable years beginning after December 31, 2010.

TAX CUTS FOR BUSINESS

ELIMINATE CAPITAL GAINS TAXATION ON INVESTMENTS IN SMALL BUSINESS STOCK

Current Law

Taxpayers other than corporations may exclude 50 percent (60 percent for certain empowerment zone businesses) of the gain from the sale of certain small business stock acquired at original issue and held for at least five years. Under the American Recovery and Reinvestment Act (ARRA), the exclusion is increased to 75 percent for stock acquired after February 17, 2009, and before January 1, 2011. The taxable portion of the gain is taxed at a maximum rate of 28 percent. Under current law, 7 percent of the excluded gain is a tax preference subject to the alternative minimum tax (AMT). For sales or exchanges in taxable years beginning after December 31, 2010, the AMT preference is scheduled to increase to 28 percent of the excluded gain on eligible stock acquired after December 31, 2000, and to 42 percent of the excluded gain on stock acquired on or before December 31, 2000.

The maximum amount of gain eligible for the exclusion by a taxpayer with respect to any corporation during any year is the greater of (1) ten times the taxpayer's basis in stock issued by the corporation and disposed of during the year, or (2) $10 million reduced by gain excluded in prior years on dispositions of the corporation's stock. To qualify as a small business, the corporation, when the stock is issued, may not have gross assets exceeding $50 million (including the proceeds of the newly issued stock) and may not be an S corporation.

The corporation also must meet certain active trade or business requirements. For example, the corporation must be engaged in a trade or business other than: one involving the performance of services in the fields of health, law, engineering, architecture, accounting, actuarial science, performing arts, consulting, athletics, financial services, brokerage services or any other trade or business where the principal asset of the trade or business is the reputation or skill of one or more employees; a banking, insurance, financing, leasing, investing or similar business; a farming business; a business involving production or extraction of items subject to depletion; or a hotel, motel, restaurant or similar business. There are limits on the amount of real property that may be held by a qualified small business, and ownership of, dealing in, or renting real property is not treated as an active trade or business.

Reasons for Change

Because the taxable portion of gain from the sale of qualified small business stock is subject to tax at a maximum of 28 percent and a percentage of the excluded gain is a preference under the AMT, the 50-percent exclusion provision provides little benefit. Increasing the exclusion would encourage and reward new investment in qualified small business stock.

Proposal

Under the proposal the percentage exclusion for qualified small business stock sold by an individual or other non-corporate taxpayer would be increased permanently to 100 percent and the AMT preference item for gain excluded under this provision would be eliminated. As under current law, the stock would have to be held for at least five years and other limitations on the section 1202 exclusion would continue to apply. The proposal would include additional documentation requirements to assure compliance with those limitations.

The proposal would be effective for qualified small business stock acquired after February 17, 2009.

MAKE RESEARCH & EXPERIMENTATION TAX CREDIT PERMANENT

Current Law

The research and experimentation (R&E) tax credit is 20 percent of qualified research expenses above a base amount. The base amount is the product of the taxpayer's "fixed base percentage" and the average of the taxpayer's gross receipts for the four preceding years. The taxpayer's fixed base percentage generally is the ratio of its research expenses to gross receipts for the 1984-88 period. The base amount cannot be less than 50 percent of the taxpayer's qualified research expenses for the taxable year. Taxpayers can elect the alternative simplified research credit (ASC), which is equal to 14 percent of qualified research expenses that exceed 50 percent of the average qualified research expenses for the three preceding taxable years. Under the ASC, the rate is reduced to 6 percent if a taxpayer has no qualified research expenses in any one of the three preceding taxable years. An election to use the ASC applies to all succeeding taxable years unless revoked with the consent of the Secretary.

The R&E tax credit also provides a credit for 20 percent of: (1) basic research payments above a base amount; and (2) all eligible payments to an energy research consortium for energy research.

The R&E tax credit expired on December 31, 2009.

Reasons for Change

The R&E tax credit encourages technological developments that are an important component of economic growth. However, uncertainty about the future availability of the R&E tax credit diminishes the incentive effect of the credit because it is difficult for taxpayers to factor the credit into decisions to invest in research projects that will not be initiated and completed prior to the credit's expiration. To improve the credit's effectiveness, the R&E tax credit should be made permanent.

Proposal

The proposal would make the R&E credit permanent, effective as of January 1, 2010.

REMOVE CELL PHONES FROM LISTED PROPERTY

Current Law

Generally, a taxpayer may claim a deduction for ordinary and necessary expenses paid or incurred in carrying on any trade or business. However, with respect to "listed property," the deduction is limited, as described below. Listed property includes any cellular telephone (or other similar telecommunications equipment), certain automobiles and computers specified by statute, and any equipment of a type generally used for purposes of entertainment, recreation, or amusement.

A deduction with respect to expenses for listed property is disallowed unless the taxpayer substantiates by adequate records or by sufficient evidence corroborating the taxpayer's own statement (A) the amount of such expense or other item, (B) the use of the listed property, (C) the business purpose of the expense or other item, and (D) the business relationship to the taxpayer of persons using the listed property. In addition, annual depreciation deductions (and any small business expensing deduction) are limited with respect to listed property not used predominantly for business purposes.

Generally, gross income includes compensation for services, including fringe benefits. An employee generally must include in gross income the fair market value of a fringe benefit (reduced by any amount paid by the employee or specifically excluded from income). The fair market value of a fringe benefit is the amount that an individual would have to pay for the particular fringe benefit in an arm's length transaction (regardless of the cost actually incurred by the employer). To the extent that an employee uses a business cell phone for personal purposes, the fair market value of such usage is includable in the employee's gross income.

Reasons for Change

The substantiation requirements with respect to listed property are burdensome for employers, employees, and the IRS. In the case of cell phones, a myriad of billing arrangements multiply the difficulty of documenting the cost of calls. Moreover, there has been a significant reduction in the cost of service since cell phones were first classified as listed property, such that the cost of accounting for personal use often exceeds the amount of any resulting income. Small businesses, which lack economies of scale in implementing systems to track costs, may be particularly burdened by the substantiation requirements. In the current economy, cell phones have become a ubiquitous device for doing business.

Proposal

Cell phones (and other similar telecommunications equipment) would no longer be classified as listed property, effectively removing the requirement of strict substantiation of use and the limitation on depreciation deductions. The fair market value of personal use of a cell phone (or other similar telecommunications equipment) provided primarily for business purposes would be excluded from gross income.

The proposal would be effective for taxable years ending after the date of enactment.

CONTINUE CERTAIN EXPIRING PROVISIONS THROUGH CALENDAR YEAR 2011

A number of temporary tax provisions are scheduled to expire before December 31, 2011. The Administration proposes to extend a number of these provisions through December 31, 2011. These provisions include the optional deduction for State and local general sales taxes, the Subpart F "active financing" and "look-through" exceptions, the exclusion from unrelated business income of certain payments to controlling exempt organizations, the modified recovery period for qualified leasehold improvements and qualified restaurant property, incentives for empowerment and community renewal zones, and several trade agreements, including the Generalized System of Preferences and the Caribbean Basin Initiative. In accordance with the President's agreement at the G-20 Summit in Pittsburgh to phase out subsidies for fossil fuels, temporary incentives provided for the production of fossil fuels would be allowed to expire as scheduled under current law.

OTHER REVENUE CHANGES AND LOOPHOLE CLOSERS

Reform Treatment of Financial Institutions and Products

IMPOSE A FINANCIAL CRISIS RESPONSIBILITY FEE

Current Law

There is no sector-specific Federal tax applied to financial firms (although these firms are subject to the general corporate income tax and potentially a wide range of excise taxes). Financial sector firms are subject to a range of fees, depending on the lines of business in which they participate. For example, banks are assessed fees by the Federal Deposit Insurance Corporation to cover the costs of insuring deposits made at these institutions.

Reasons for Change

Excessive risk undertaken by major financial firms was a significant cause of the recent financial crisis. Extraordinary steps were taken by the Federal government to inject funds into the financial system, guarantee certain types of securities, and purchase securities from weakened firms. The law which enabled some of these actions and which created the Troubled Asset Relief Program (TARP) required that the President propose an assessment on the financial sector to pay back the costs of these extraordinary actions. This fee is intended to meet that statutory requirement. The fee would also provide a deterrent against excessive leverage for the largest financial firms.

Proposal

The Financial Crisis Responsibility Fee is to be assessed on certain liabilities of the largest firms in the financial sector. Specific components of the proposal are described here.

Firms Subject to the Fee: The fee would be applied to banks, thrifts, bank and thrift holding companies, brokers, and securities dealers. U.S. companies owning or controlling these types of entities as of January 14, 2010 also would be subject to the fee. Firms with consolidated assets of less than $50 billion would not be subject to the fee for the period when their assets are below this threshold.

Base of fee: In general, the assessable base of the fee would include the worldwide consolidated liabilities of U.S. financial firms. Financial firms not based in the United States would be subject to the fee based on the liabilities of their U.S. subsidiaries. The fee base would include a broad set of liabilities with a few designated exceptions. For example, for firms that own depository institutions, FDIC-assessed deposits would not be subject to the fee. Similarly, for insurance companies, certain policy-related liabilities would not be subject to the fee. In addition, adjustments would be provided to prevent avoidance and to appropriately treat less risky activities, such as lending against certain high quality collateral.

Computing Covered Liability Amounts: For financial firms, generally covered liabilities would be determined using balance sheet information filed with the appropriate Federal or State regulators.

Fee Rates: The rate of the fee applied to covered liabilities would be approximately 15 basis points.

Filing and Payment Requirements: Entities subject to the fee would report it on their annual Federal income tax return. Estimated payments of the fee would be made on the same schedule as estimated income tax payments.

Effective Date: The fee would be effective as of July 1, 2010. Thus, calendar year taxpayers would pay the fee with respect to two quarters of the year when filing their returns for 2010.

REQUIRE ACCRUAL OF INCOME ON FORWARD SALE OF CORPORATE STOCK

Current Law

A corporation generally does not recognize gain or loss on the issuance or repurchase of its own stock. Thus, a corporation does not recognize gain or loss on the forward sale of its own stock. A corporation sells its stock forward by agreeing to issue its stock in the future in exchange for consideration to be paid in the future.

Although a corporation does not recognize gain or loss on the issuance of its own stock, a corporation does recognize interest income upon the current sale of any stock (including its own) for deferred payment.

Reasons for Change

There is little substantive difference between a corporate issuer's current sale of its stock for deferred payment and an issuer's forward sale of the same stock. The only difference between the two transactions is the timing of the stock issuance. In a current sale, the stock is issued at the inception of the transaction, but in a forward sale, the stock is issued at the time the deferred payment is received. In both cases, a portion of the deferred payment economically compensates the corporation for the time value of deferring receipt of the payment. It is inappropriate to treat these two transactions differently.

Proposal

The proposal would require a corporation that enters into a forward contract to issue its stock to treat a portion of the payment on the forward issuance as a payment of interest.

The proposal would be effective for forward contracts entered into after December 31, 2011.

REQUIRE ORDINARY TREATMENT OF INCOME FROM DAY-TO-DAY DEALER ACTIVITIES FOR CERTAIN DEALERS IN COMMODITIES, DERIVATIVES AND OTHER SECURITIES

Current Law

Under current law, certain dealers treat the income from some of their day-to-day dealer activities as capital gain. This special rule applies to certain transactions in section 1256 contracts by commodities dealers (within the meaning of section 1402(i) (2) (B)), commodities derivatives dealers (within the meaning of section 1221(b) (1) (A)), dealers in securities (within the meaning of section 475(c) (1)), and options dealers (within the meaning of section 1256(g) (8)). Under section 1256, these dealers treat 60 percent of their income (or loss) from their dealer activities in section 1256 contracts as long-term capital gain (or loss) and 40 percent of their income (or loss) from these dealer activities as short-term capital gain (or loss). Dealers in other types of property generally treat the income from their day-to-day dealer activities as ordinary income.

Reasons for Change

There is no reason to treat dealers in commodities, commodities derivatives dealers, dealers in securities, and dealers in options differently from dealers in other types of property. Dealers earn their income from their day-to-day dealer activities, and this income should be taxed at ordinary rates.

Proposal

The proposal would require dealers in commodities, commodities derivatives dealers, dealers in securities, and dealers in options to treat the income from their day-to-day dealer activities in section 1256 contracts as ordinary in character, not capital.

The proposal would be effective for taxable years beginning after the date of enactment.

MODIFY DEFINITION OF "CONTROL" FOR PURPOSES OF SECTION 249

Current Law

In general, if a corporation repurchases a debt instrument that is convertible into its stock, or into stock of a corporation in control of, or controlled by, the corporation, section 249 may disallow or limit the issuer's deduction for a premium paid to repurchase the debt instrument. For this purpose, "control" is determined by reference to section 368(c), which encompasses only direct relationships (e.g., a parent corporation and its wholly-owned, first-tier subsidiary).

Reasons for Change

The definition of "control" in section 249 is unnecessarily restrictive and has allowed the limitation in section 249 to be too easily avoided. Indirect control relationships (e.g., a parent corporation and a second-tier subsidiary) present the same economic identity of interests as direct control relationships and should be treated in a similar manner.

Proposal

Under the proposal, the definition of "control" in section 249(b) (2) would be amended to incorporate indirect control relationships of the nature described in section 1563(a) (1).

The proposal would be effective on the date of enactment.

Reinstate Superfund Taxes

REINSTATE SUPERFUND EXCISE TAXES

Current Law

The following Superfund excise taxes were imposed before January 1, 1996:

(1) An excise tax on domestic crude oil and on imported petroleum products at a rate of $0.097 per barrel;

(2) An excise tax on listed hazardous chemicals at a rate that varied from $0.22 to $4.87 per ton; and

(3) An excise tax on imported substances that use as materials in their manufacture or production one or more of the hazardous chemicals subject to the excise tax described in (2) above.

Amounts equivalent to the revenues from these taxes were dedicated to the Hazardous Substance Superfund Trust Fund (the Superfund Trust Fund). Amounts in the Superfund Trust Fund are available for expenditures incurred in connection with releases or threats of releases of hazardous substances into the environment under specified provisions of the Comprehensive Environmental Response, Compensation, and Liability Act of 1980 (as amended).

Reasons for Change

The Superfund excise taxes should be reinstated because of the continuing need for funds to remedy damages caused by releases of hazardous substances.

Proposal

The three Superfund excise taxes would be reinstated for periods after December 31, 2010. The taxes would sunset after December 31, 2020.

REINSTATE SUPERFUND ENVIRONMENTAL INCOME TAX

Current Law

For taxable years beginning before January 1, 1996, a corporate environmental income tax was imposed at a rate of 0.12 percent on the amount by which the modified alternative minimum taxable income of a corporation exceeded $2 million. Modified alternative minimum taxable income was defined as a corporation's alternative minimum taxable income, determined without regard to the alternative minimum tax net operating loss deduction and the deduction for the corporate environmental income tax.

The tax was dedicated to the Hazardous Substance Superfund Trust Fund (the Superfund Trust Fund). Amounts in the Superfund Trust Fund are available for expenditures incurred in connection with releases or threats of releases of hazardous substances into the environment under specified provisions of the Comprehensive Environmental Response, Compensation, and Liability Act of 1980 (as amended).

Reasons for Change

The corporate environmental income tax should be reinstated because of the continuing need for funds to remedy damages caused by releases of hazardous substances.

Proposal

The corporate environmental income tax would be reinstated for taxable years beginning after December 31, 2010. The tax would sunset for taxable years beginning after December 31, 2020.

MAKE UNEMPLOYMENT INSURANCE SURTAX PERMANENT

Current Law

The Federal Unemployment Tax Act (FUTA) currently imposes a Federal payroll tax on employers of 6.2 percent of the first $7,000 paid annually to each employee. The tax funds a portion of the Federal/State unemployment benefits system. This 6.2 percent rate includes a temporary surtax of 0.2 percent (discussed below). States also impose an unemployment tax on employers. Employers in States that meet certain Federal requirements are allowed a credit for State unemployment taxes of up to 5.4 percent, making the minimum net Federal tax rate 0.8 percent. Generally, Federal and State unemployment taxes are collected quarterly and deposited in Federal trust fund accounts.

In 1976, Congress passed a temporary surtax of 0.2 percent of taxable wages to be added to the permanent FUTA tax rate. Thus, the current 0.8 percent net FUTA tax rate has two components: a permanent tax rate of 0.6 percent and a temporary surtax rate of 0.2 percent. The surtax has been extended several times, most recently through June 30, 2011.

Reasons for Change

Extending the surtax will support the continued solvency of the Federal unemployment trust funds.

Proposal

The proposal would make the 0.2 percent surtax permanent.

REPEAL LIFO METHOD OF ACCOUNTING FOR INVENTORIES

Current Law

A taxpayer with inventory may determine the value of its inventory and its cost of goods sold using a number of different methods. The most prevalent method is the first-in, first-out (FIFO) method, which matches current sales with the costs of the earliest acquired (or manufactured) inventory items. As an alternative, a taxpayer may elect to use the last-in, first-out (LIFO) method, which treats the most recently acquired (or manufactured) goods as having been sold during the year. The LIFO method can provide a tax benefit for a taxpayer facing rising inventory costs, since the cost of goods sold under this method is based on more recent, higher inventory values, resulting in lower taxable income. If inventory levels fall during the year, however, a LIFO taxpayer must include lower-cost LIFO inventory values (reflecting one or more prior-year inventory accumulations) in the cost of goods sold, and its taxable income will be correspondingly higher. To be eligible to elect LIFO for tax purposes, a taxpayer must use LIFO for financial accounting purposes.

Reasons for Change

The repeal of the LIFO method would eliminate a tax deferral opportunity available to taxpayers that hold inventories, the costs of which increase over time. In addition, LIFO repeal would simplify the Code by removing a complex and burdensome accounting method that has been the source of controversy between taxpayers and the IRS.

International Financial Reporting Standards do not permit the use of the LIFO method, and their adoption by the Securities and Exchange Commission would cause violations of the current LIFO book/tax conformity requirement. Repealing LIFO would remove this possible impediment to the implementation of these standards in the United States.

Proposal

The proposal would not allow the use of the LIFO inventory accounting method for Federal income tax purposes. Taxpayers that currently use the LIFO method would be required to write up their beginning LIFO inventory to its FIFO value in the first taxable year beginning after December 31, 2011. However, this one-time increase in gross income would be taken into account ratably over ten years, beginning with the first taxable year beginning after December 31, 2011.

REPEAL GAIN LIMITATION FOR DIVIDENDS RECEIVED IN REORGANIZATION EXCHANGES

Current Law

Under section 356(a)(1), if as part of a reorganization transaction an exchanging shareholder receives in exchange for its stock of the target corporation both stock and property that cannot be received without the recognition of gain (often referred to as "boot"), the exchanging shareholder is required to recognize gain equal to the lesser of the gain realized in the exchange or the amount of boot received (commonly referred to as the "boot within gain" limitation). Further, under section 356(a)(2), if the exchange has the effect of the distribution of a dividend, then all or part of the gain recognized by the exchanging shareholder is treated as a dividend to the extent of the shareholder's ratable share of the corporation's earnings and profits. The remainder of the gain (if any) is treated as gain from the exchange of property.

Reasons for Change

There is not a significant policy reason to vary the treatment of a distribution that otherwise qualifies as a dividend by reference to whether it is received in the normal course of a corporation's operations or is instead received as part of a reorganization exchange. Thus, repealing the boot-within-gain limitation for an exchange that has the effect of the distribution of a dividend will provide more uniform treatment for dividends that is less dependent on context. Moreover, in cross-border reorganizations, the boot-within-gain limitation can permit U.S. shareholders to repatriate previously-untaxed earnings and profits of foreign subsidiaries with minimal U.S. tax consequences. For example, if the exchanging shareholder's stock in the target corporation has little or no built-in gain at the time of the exchange, the shareholder will recognize minimal gain even if the exchange has the effect of the distribution of a dividend and/or a significant amount (or all) of the consideration received in the exchange is boot. This result applies even if the corporation has previously untaxed earnings and profits equal to or greater than the boot. This result is inconsistent with the principle that previously untaxed earnings and profits of a foreign subsidiary should be subject to U.S. tax upon repatriation.

Proposal

The proposal would repeal the boot-within-gain limitation of current law in the case of any reorganization transaction if the exchange has the effect of the distribution of a dividend, as determined under section 356(a)(2).

The proposal would be effective for taxable years beginning after December 31, 2010.

Reform the U.S. International Tax System

DEFER DEDUCTION OF INTEREST EXPENSE RELATED TO DEFERRED INCOME

Current Law

Taxpayers generally may deduct ordinary and necessary expenses paid or incurred in carrying on any trade or business. The Internal Revenue Code and the regulations thereunder contain detailed rules regarding allocation and apportionment of expenses for computing taxable income from sources within and without the United States. Under current rules, a U.S. person that incurs interest expense properly allocable and apportioned to foreign-source income may deduct those expenses even if the expenses exceed the taxpayer's gross foreign-source income or if the taxpayer earns no foreign-source income. For example, a U.S. person that incurs debt to acquire stock of a foreign corporation is generally permitted to deduct currently the interest expense from the acquisition indebtedness even if no income is derived currently from such stock. Current law includes provisions that may require a U.S. person to recapture as U.S.-source income the amount by which foreign-source expenses exceed foreign-source income for a taxable year. However, if in a taxable year the U.S. person earns sufficient foreign-source income of the same statutory grouping in which the stock of the foreign corporation is classified, expenses, such as interest expense, properly allocated and apportioned to the stock of the foreign corporation may not be subject to recapture in a subsequent taxable year.

Reasons for Change

The ability to deduct expenses from overseas investments while deferring U.S. tax on the income from the investment may cause U.S. businesses to shift their investments and jobs overseas, harming our domestic economy.

Proposal

The proposal would defer the deduction of interest expense that is properly allocated and apportioned to a taxpayer's foreign-source income that is not currently subject to U.S. tax. For purposes of the proposal, foreign-source income earned by a taxpayer through a branch would be considered currently subject to U.S. tax, thus the proposal would not apply to interest expense properly allocated and apportioned to such income. Other directly earned foreign source income (for example, royalty income) would be similarly treated.

For purposes of the proposal, the amount of a taxpayer's interest expense that is properly allocated and apportioned to foreign-source income would generally be determined under current Treasury regulations. The Treasury Department, however, will revise existing Treasury regulations and propose such other statutory changes as necessary to prevent inappropriate decreases in the amount of interest expense that is allocated and apportioned to foreign-source income.

Deferred interest expense would be deductible in a subsequent tax year in proportion to the amount of the previously deferred foreign-source income that is subject to U.S. tax during that subsequent tax year. Treasury regulations may modify the manner in which a taxpayer can deduct previously deferred interest expenses in certain cases.

The proposal would be effective for taxable years beginning after December 31, 2010.

FOREIGN TAX CREDIT REFORM: DETERMINE THE FOREIGN TAX CREDIT ON A POOLING BASIS

Current Law

Section 901 provides that, subject to certain limitations, a taxpayer may choose to claim a credit against its U.S. income tax liability for income, war profits, and excess profits taxes paid or accrued during the taxable year to any foreign country or any possession of the United States. Under section 902, a domestic corporation is deemed to have paid the foreign taxes paid by certain foreign subsidiaries from which it receives a dividend (the deemed paid foreign tax credit). The foreign tax credit is limited to an amount equal to the pre-credit U.S. tax on the taxpayer's foreign-source income. This foreign tax credit limitation is applied separately to foreign-source income in each of the separate categories described in section 904(d), i.e., the passive category and general category.

Reasons for Change

The purpose of the foreign tax credit is to mitigate the potential for double taxation when U.S. taxpayers are subject to foreign taxes on their foreign-source income. The reduction to two foreign tax credit limitation categories, for passive category income and general category income under the American Jobs Creation Act of 2004, enhanced U.S. taxpayers' ability to reduce the residual U.S. tax on foreign-source income through "cross-crediting."

Proposal

Under the proposal, a U.S. taxpayer would determine its deemed paid foreign tax credit on a consolidated basis based on the aggregate foreign taxes and earnings and profits of all of the foreign subsidiaries with respect to which the U.S. taxpayer can claim a deemed paid foreign tax credit (including lower tier subsidiaries described in section 902(b)). The deemed paid foreign tax credit for a taxable year would be determined based on the amount of the consolidated earnings and profits of the foreign subsidiaries repatriated to the U.S. taxpayer in that taxable year. The Secretary would be granted authority to issue any Treasury regulations necessary to carry out the purposes of the proposal.

The proposal would be effective for taxable years beginning after December 31, 2010.

FOREIGN TAX CREDIT REFORM: PREVENT SPLITTING OF FOREIGN INCOME AND FOREIGN TAXES

Current Law

Section 901 provides that, subject to certain limitations, a taxpayer may choose to claim a credit against its U.S. income tax liability for income, war profits, and excess profits taxes paid or accrued during the taxable year to any foreign country or any possession of the United States. Under current law, the person considered to have paid the foreign tax is the person on whom foreign law imposes legal liability for such tax.

Reasons for Change

Current law permits inappropriate separation of creditable foreign taxes from the associated foreign income in certain cases such as those involving hybrid arrangements.

Proposal

In the case of foreign taxes with respect to which a taxpayer claims credit under section 901, the proposal would adopt a matching rule to prevent the separation of creditable foreign taxes from the associated foreign income. In general, the proposal would allow a credit for such foreign taxes when and to the extent the associated foreign income is subject to U.S. tax in the hands of the taxpayer claiming the credit. This proposal would apply in addition to the section 902 "pooling" proposal described in this document. The Secretary would be granted authority to issue any regulations necessary to carry out the purposes of the proposal.

The proposal would be effective for taxable years beginning after December 31, 2010.

TAX CURRENTLY EXCESS RETURNS ASSOCIATED WITH TRANSFERS OF INTANGIBLES OFFSHORE

Current Law

Section 482 authorizes the Secretary to distribute, apportion, or allocate gross income, deductions, credits, and other allowances between or among two or more organizations, trades, or businesses under common ownership or control whenever "necessary in order to prevent evasion of taxes or clearly to reflect the income of any of such organizations, trades, or businesses." The regulations under Section 482 provide that the standard to be applied is that of unrelated persons dealing at arm's length. In the case of transfers of intangible assets, section 482 further provides that the income with respect to the transaction must be commensurate with the income attributable to the intangible assets transferred.

Reasons for Change

The potential tax savings from transactions between related parties, especially with regard to transfers of intangible assets to low-taxed affiliates, puts significant pressure on the enforcement and effective application of transfer pricing rules. There is evidence indicating that income shifting through transfers of intangibles to low-taxed affiliates has resulted in a significant erosion of the U.S. tax base.

Proposal

Under the proposal, if a U.S. person transfers an intangible from the United States to a related controlled foreign corporation that is subject to a low foreign effective tax rate in circumstances that evidence excessive income shifting, then an amount equal to the excessive return would be treated as subpart F income in a separate foreign tax credit limitation basket.

The proposal would be effective for taxable years beginning after December 31, 2010.

LIMIT SHIFTING OF INCOME THROUGH INTANGIBLE PROPERTY TRANSFERS

Current Law

Section 482 permits the Secretary to distribute, apportion, or allocate gross income, deductions, credits, and other allowances between or among two or more organizations, trades, or businesses under common ownership or control whenever "necessary in order to prevent evasion of taxes or clearly to reflect the income of any of such organizations, trades, or businesses." Section 482 also provides that in the case of any transfer of intangible assets, the income with respect to the transaction must be commensurate with the income attributable to the intangible assets transferred. Further, under section 367(d), if a U.S. person transfers intangible property (as defined in section 936(h)(3)(B)) to a foreign corporation in certain nonrecognition transactions, the U.S. person is treated as selling the intangible property for a series of payments contingent on the productivity, use, or disposition of the property that are commensurate with the transferee's income from the property. The payments generally continue annually over the useful life of the property.

Reasons for Change

Controversy often arises concerning the value of intangible property transferred between related persons and the scope of the intangible property subject to sections 482 and 367(d). This lack of clarity may result in the inappropriate avoidance of U.S. tax and misuse of the rules applicable to transfers of intangible property to foreign persons.

Proposal

To prevent inappropriate shifting of income outside the United States, the proposal would clarify the definition of intangible property for purposes of sections 367(d) and 482 to include workforce in place, goodwill and going concern value. The proposal also would clarify that where multiple intangible properties are transferred, the Commissioner may value the intangible properties on an aggregate basis where that achieves a more reliable result. In addition, the proposal would clarify that the Commissioner may value intangible property taking into consideration the prices or profits that the controlled taxpayer could have realized by choosing a realistic alternative to the controlled transaction undertaken.

The proposal would be effective for taxable years beginning after December 31, 2010.

DISALLOW THE DEDUCTION FOR EXCESS NONTAXED REINSURANCE PREMIUMS PAID TO AFFILIATES

Current Law

Insurance companies are generally allowed a deduction for premiums paid for reinsurance. If the reinsurance transaction results in a transfer of reserves and reserve assets to the reinsurer, potential tax liability for earnings on those assets is generally shifted to the reinsurer as well. While insurance income of a controlled foreign corporation is generally subject to current U.S. taxation, insurance income of a foreign-owned foreign company that is not engaged in a trade or business in the United States is not subject to U.S. income tax. Reinsurance policies issued by foreign reinsurers with respect to U.S. risks are generally subject to an excise tax equal to one percent of the premiums paid, unless waived by treaty.

Reasons for Change

Reinsurance transactions with affiliates that are not subject to U.S. Federal income tax on insurance income can result in substantial U.S. tax advantages over similar transactions with entities that are subject to tax in the United States. The excise tax on reinsurance policies issued by foreign reinsurers is not always sufficient to offset this tax advantage. These tax advantages create incentives for foreign-owned domestic insurance companies to reinsure direct insurance of U.S. risks with foreign affiliates to an extent that would not occur between unrelated parties acting at arm's length. It is inappropriate to allow a deduction for reinsurance premiums paid under such circumstances.

Proposal

Under the proposal, a U.S. insurance company would be denied a deduction for certain reinsurance premiums paid to affiliated foreign reinsurance companies with respect to U.S. risks insured by the insurance company or its U.S. affiliates. The U.S. insurance company would not be allowed a deduction to the extent that (1) the foreign reinsurers (or their parent companies) are not subject to U.S. income tax with respect to premiums received and (2) the amount of reinsurance premiums (net of ceding commissions) paid to foreign reinsurers exceeds 50 percent of the total direct insurance premiums received by the U.S. insurance company and its U.S. affiliates for a line of business.

The proposal provides that a foreign corporation that is paid a premium from an affiliate that would otherwise be denied a deduction under this provision may elect to treat those premiums and the associated investment income as income effectively connected with the conduct of a trade or business in the United States.

The provision is effective for taxable years beginning after December 31, 2010.

LIMIT EARNINGS STRIPPING BY EXPATRIATED ENTITIES

Section 163(j) limits the deductibility of certain interest paid by a corporation to related persons. The limitation applies to a corporation that fails a debt-to-equity safe harbor (greater than 1.5 to 1) and that has net interest expense in excess of 50 percent of adjusted taxable income (computed by adding back net interest expense, depreciation, amortization and depletion, and any net operating loss deduction). Disallowed interest expense may be carried forward indefinitely for deduction in a subsequent year. In addition, the corporation's excess limitation for a tax year (i.e., the amount by which 50 percent of adjusted taxable income exceeds net interest expense) may be carried forward to the three subsequent tax years.

Section 7874 provides special rules for expatriated entities and the acquiring foreign corporations. The rules apply to certain defined transactions in which a U.S. parent company (the expatriated entity) is essentially replaced with a foreign parent (the surrogate foreign corporation). The tax treatment of an expatriated entity and a surrogate foreign corporation varies depending on the extent of continuity of shareholder ownership following the transaction. The surrogate foreign corporation is treated as a domestic corporation for all purposes of the Code if shareholder ownership continuity is at least 80 percent (by vote or value). If shareholder ownership continuity is at least 60 percent, but less than 80 percent, the surrogate foreign corporation is treated as a foreign corporation but any applicable corporate-level income or gain required to be recognized by the expatriated entity generally cannot be offset by tax attributes. Section 7874 generally applies to transactions occurring on or after March 4, 2003.

Reasons for Change

Under current law, opportunities are available to reduce inappropriately the U.S. tax on income earned from U.S. operations through the use of foreign related-party debt. In its 2007 study of earnings stripping, the Treasury Department found strong evidence of the use of such techniques by expatriated entities. Consequently, amending the rules of section 163(j) for expatriated entities is necessary to prevent these inappropriate income-reduction opportunities.

Proposal

The proposal would revise section 163(j) to tighten the limitation on the deductibility of interest paid by an expatriated entity to related persons. The current law debt-to-equity safe harbor would be eliminated. The 50 percent adjusted taxable income threshold for the limitation would be reduced to 25 percent. The carryforward for disallowed interest would be limited to ten years and the carryforward of excess limitation would be eliminated.

An expatriated entity would be defined by applying the rules of section 7874 and the regulations thereunder as if section 7874 were applicable for taxable years beginning after July 10, 1989. This special rule would not apply, however, if the surrogate foreign corporation is treated as a domestic corporation under section 7874.

The proposal would be effective for taxable years beginning after December 31, 2010.

REPEAL 80/20 COMPANY RULES

Current Law

Dividends and interest paid by a domestic corporation are generally U.S.-source income to the recipient and are generally subject to gross basis withholding tax if paid to a foreign person. A limited exception to these general rules applies with respect to a domestic corporation (a so-called "80/20" company) if at least 80 percent of the corporation's gross income during a three-year testing period is foreign-source and attributable to the active conduct of a foreign trade or business. Look-through rules apply to determine the character of certain income of the 80/20 company for this purpose.

Reasons for Change

The 80/20 company provisions can be manipulated and should be repealed.

Proposal

The proposal would repeal the 80/20 company provisions under current law.

The proposal would be effective for taxable years beginning after December 31, 2010.

PREVENT THE AVOIDANCE OF DIVIDEND WITHHOLDING TAXES

Current Law

A withholding agent generally must withhold a tax of 30 percent from the gross amount of all U.S.-source fixed or determinable annual or periodical (FDAP) income, profits, or gains of a nonresident alien individual, foreign corporation, or foreign partnership. In general, dividends paid with respect to the stock of a domestic corporation are U.S.-source dividends. Thus, foreign investors holding stock in domestic corporations are generally subject to 30-percent tax on dividends paid with respect to that stock. This rate may be reduced where the dividends are paid to a resident of a jurisdiction with which the United States has entered into a tax treaty.

The source of income from a notional principal contract is generally determined based on the residence of the investor. As a result, substitute dividend payments made to a foreign investor with respect to an equity swap referencing U.S. equities are treated as foreign-source and are therefore not subject to U.S. withholding tax.

Reasons for Change

Foreign portfolio investors seeking to benefit from the appreciation in value and dividends paid with respect to the stock of a domestic corporation are not limited to holding stock in the corporation. Instead, such an investor can enter into an equity swap. The U.S. tax consequences of these two alternative investments differ significantly. By entering into equity swaps, foreign portfolio investors receive the economic benefit of dividends paid and appreciation in value with respect to U.S. stock without being subject to gross-basis withholding tax.

Proposal

Income earned by foreign persons with respect to equity swaps that reference U.S. equities would be treated as U.S.-source to the extent that the income is attributable to (or calculated by reference to) dividends paid by a domestic corporation. An exception to this source rule would apply to swaps which are unlikely to reflect avoidance of U.S. gross-basis taxation. The proposal would (1) ensure that economically equivalent transactions are subject to similar tax treatment, and (2) prevent avoidance of dividend withholding taxes by reforming the existing rules applicable to substitute dividends in a securities loan or a sale-repurchase transaction, while minimizing instances of over-withholding. The Treasury Department would be given regulatory authority to provide additional exceptions to implement the purpose of these rules.

The proposal would be effective for payments made after December 31, 2010.

MODIFY THE TAX RULES FOR DUAL CAPACITY TAXPAYERS

Current Law

Section 901 provides that, subject to certain limitations, a taxpayer may choose to claim a credit against its U.S. income tax liability for income, war profits, and excess profits taxes paid or accrued during the taxable year to any foreign country or any possession of the United States. To be a creditable tax, a foreign levy must be substantially equivalent to an income tax under United States tax principles, regardless of the label attached to the levy under law. Under current Treasury regulations, a foreign levy is a tax if it is a compulsory payment under the authority of a foreign government to levy taxes and is not compensation for a specific economic benefit provided by the foreign country. Taxpayers that are subject to a foreign levy and that also receive a specific economic benefit from the levying country (dual capacity taxpayers) may not credit the portion of the foreign levy paid for the specific economic benefit. The current Treasury regulations provide that, if a foreign country has a generally-imposed income tax, the dual capacity taxpayer may treat as a creditable tax the portion of the levy that application of the generally imposed income tax would yield (provided that the levy otherwise constitutes an income tax or an in lieu of tax). The balance of the levy is treated as compensation for the specific economic benefit. If the foreign country does not generally impose an income tax, the portion of the payment that does not exceed the applicable federal tax rate applied to net income is treated as a creditable tax. A foreign tax is treated as generally imposed even if it applies only to persons who are not residents or nationals of that country.

There is no separate section 904 foreign tax credit basket for oil and gas income. However, under section 907, the amount of creditable foreign taxes imposed on foreign oil and gas income is limited in any year to the applicable U.S. tax on that income.

Reasons for Change

The purpose of the foreign tax credit is to mitigate double taxation of income by the United States and a foreign country. When a payment is made to a foreign country in exchange for a specific economic benefit, there is no double taxation. Current law recognizes the distinction between a payment of creditable taxes and a payment in exchange for a specific economic benefit but fails to achieve the appropriate split between the two when a single payment is made in a case where, for example, a foreign country imposes a levy only on oil and gas income, or imposes a higher levy on oil and gas income as compared to other income.

Proposal

In the case of a dual capacity taxpayer, the proposal would allow the taxpayer to treat as a creditable tax the portion of a foreign levy that does not exceed the foreign levy that the taxpayer would pay if it were not a dual-capacity taxpayer. The proposal would replace the current regulatory provisions, including the safe harbor, that apply to determine the amount of a foreign levy paid by a dual-capacity taxpayer that qualifies as a creditable tax. The proposal also would convert the special foreign tax credit limitation rules of section 907 into a separate category within section 904 for foreign oil and gas income. The proposal would yield to United States treaty obligations to the extent that they allow a credit for taxes paid or accrued on certain oil or gas income.

The proposal would be effective for taxable years beginning after December 31, 2010.

Combat Under-Reporting of Income on Accounts and Entities in Offshore Jurisdictions

For too long, some Americans have evaded their taxpaying responsibilities by hiding unreported income in a foreign bank account, trust, or corporation. To reduce such evasion, the Administration is proposing a series of measures to strengthen the information reporting and withholding systems that support U.S. taxation of income earned or held through offshore accounts or entities.

REQUIRE INCREASED REPORTING ON CERTAIN FOREIGN ACCOUNTS

Current Law

A withholding agent generally must withhold tax at a rate of 30 percent from the gross amount of all U.S.-source fixed or determinable annual or periodical gains, profits, or income (FDAP income) of a nonresident alien individual or foreign entity. This 30-percent withholding tax may be reduced or eliminated pursuant to certain statutory provisions or pursuant to the terms of a tax treaty. A payor is generally required to withhold tax at a rate of 28 percent on a reportable payment made to a U.S. non-exempt recipient if the payee fails to provide a taxpayer identification number or fails to certify, when required, that the payee is not subject to backup withholding, or the payor is notified by the IRS or a broker that the payee is subject to backup withholding.

To determine whether the recipient of a payment is exempt from withholding tax or eligible for a reduced rate, withholding agents generally must rely on beneficial ownership documentation provided by the payee certifying that the payee is entitled to an exemption from withholding tax or a reduced rate of withholding tax under a Code provision or relevant tax treaty. In general, withholding agents are entitled to rely on the self-certification they receive absent actual knowledge or reason to know that the information provided is incorrect or unreliable. In the case of payments made through an intermediary, the intermediary generally provides to the withholding agent the appropriate documentation on behalf of the payment's beneficial owners.

Treasury regulations specifically address certification, documentation, withholding, and reporting of payments to U.S. and foreign persons through foreign financial institutions (FFIs). FFIs may contract with the IRS to operate according to a set of withholding and reporting rules under the so-called "qualified intermediary" (QI) program. QIs agree to collect identifying documentation from their customers, file withholding tax returns and information returns, and submit to periodic audits performed by external auditors supervised by IRS examiners. QIs may furnish a withholding certificate to a withholding agent in lieu of transmitting to the withholding agent documentation for persons for whom the QI receives the payment and, in the case of U.S. non-exempt recipients, may assume primary Form 1099 reporting and backup withholding responsibility.

If a QI assumes primary Form 1099 reporting and backup withholding responsibility with respect to accounts held by U.S. persons, such reporting may be limited to certain income earned through those accounts. Further, a QI that assumes primary Form 1099 reporting and backup withholding responsibility with respect to U.S. persons is not required to assume that responsibility for all accounts. Moreover, in the case of financial institutions that are part of a controlled group, one member of the controlled group may contract to be a QI while other members of the controlled group do not, and thus accounts and clients may be divided between commonly controlled QI and non-QI institutions.

Brokers are generally required to withhold tax at a rate of 28 percent on certain reportable payments made to a U.S. non-exempt recipient if the payee fails to provide a taxpayer identification number or fails to certify that the payee is not subject to backup withholding, or the payor is notified by the IRS or a broker that the payee is subject to backup withholding. Reportable payments include the gross proceeds from certain transactions effected by brokers for their customers. A broker is exempt from reporting a payment (and thus backup withholding) where the broker can, prior to payment, associate the payment with documentation upon which it can rely to either treat the customer as a foreign beneficial owner, or treat the payment as made or presumed to be made to a foreign payee. With respect to payments through foreign intermediaries that are not qualified intermediaries (nonqualified intermediaries), brokers may rely on the beneficial owner's self-certification of non-U.S. status passed on by the nonqualified intermediary to determine whether certain third-party information reporting, and therefore backup withholding, may be required.

Reasons for Change

Strengthening the withholding and reporting rules under which FFIs operate with respect to U.S. persons will help to ensure that U.S. persons are properly paying tax on income earned through foreign accounts and that proper withholding tax applies with respect to foreign persons. In order to facilitate operation of this strengthened reporting and withholding program, a list of compliant FFIs must be made publicly available.

Proposal

Under the proposal, a withholding agent would withhold tax at a rate of 30 percent on payments to a FFI (including certain entities engaged primarily in the business of investing, reinvesting, or trading in securities, partnership interests, commodities, or any interests in the foregoing) of U.S.-source FDAP income and gross proceeds from the sale of any property of a type which can produce U.S.-source interest or dividends, unless the FFI has entered into an agreement with the IRS. The agreement would require the FFI to identify accounts (including debt and equity securities issued by the FFI that are not regularly traded on an established securities market) held at such FFI or at an FFI in the same expanded affiliated group by specified U.S. persons or by foreign entities in which a specified United States person owns, directly or indirectly, an interest of more than 10 percent (a United States owned foreign entity). The FFI would be required to report the name, address, and taxpayer identification number (TIN) of the U.S. account holder (or each substantial U.S. owner of the United States owned foreign entity account holder), the account balance or value, and the gross receipts and gross withdrawals or payments from the account. Instead of reporting the account balance and the gross receipts and gross withdrawals or payments from the account, a FFI may elect to report such information as such FFI would be required to report under sections 6041, 6042, 6045, and 6049 if such FFI were a United States person and each holder of such accounts that is a specified United States person or a United States owned foreign entity were a natural person and citizen of the United States.

This proposal would not apply to a payment if the beneficial owner is a foreign government, an international organization, a foreign central bank, or any other class of persons that the Treasury Department concludes presents a low risk of tax evasion. The Treasury Department would be authorized to issue regulations to implement the purposes of this proposal. The rules would be designed so as not to disrupt ordinary and customary market transactions. Foreign beneficial owners of payments (other than FFIs that do not qualify for the benefits of an income tax treaty with the United States) that are subject to withholding tax in excess of their income tax liability as a result of this proposal would be permitted to apply for a refund of any excess tax withheld.

The proposal would be effective beginning after December 31, 2012.

REQUIRE INCREASED REPORTING WITH RESPECT TO CERTAIN RECIPIENTS OF FDAP INCOME OR GROSS PROCEEDS

Current Law

In general, payments of U.S.-source fixed or determinable annual or periodical gains, profits, or income (FDAP income) to nonresident alien individuals and foreign entities are subject to withholding tax at a rate of 30 percent. This 30 percent withholding tax may be reduced or eliminated pursuant to certain statutory provisions or pursuant to the terms of a tax treaty.

To determine whether the recipient of a payment is exempt from withholding tax or eligible for a reduced rate, withholding agents generally must rely on beneficial ownership documentation provided by the payee certifying that the payee is entitled to an exemption from withholding tax or a reduced rate of withholding tax under a Code provision or relevant tax treaty. In general, withholding agents are entitled to rely on the self-certification they receive absent actual knowledge or reason to know that the information provided is incorrect or unreliable. In the case of payments made through an intermediary, the intermediary generally provides to the withholding agent the appropriate documentation on behalf of the payment's beneficial owners.

Brokers are generally required to withhold tax at a rate of 28 percent on certain reportable payments made to a U.S. non-exempt recipient if the payee fails to provide a taxpayer identification number (TIN) or fails to certify that the payee is not subject to backup withholding, or the payor is notified by the IRS or a broker that the payee is subject to backup withholding. Reportable payments include the gross proceeds from certain transactions effected by brokers for their customers. A broker is exempt from reporting a payment (and thus backup withholding) where the broker can, prior to payment, associate the payment with documentation upon which it can rely to either treat the customer as a foreign beneficial owner, or treat the payment as made or presumed to be made to a foreign payee. With respect to payments through foreign intermediaries that are not qualified intermediaries (nonqualified intermediaries), brokers may rely on the beneficial owner's self-certification of non-U.S. status passed on by the nonqualified intermediary to determine whether certain third-party information reporting, and therefore backup withholding, may be required.

Reasons for Change

Persons that are not entitled to an exemption from withholding tax or a reduced rate of withholding tax may arrange to receive payments through entities (other than foreign financial institutions) that appear to qualify for an exemption or a reduced rate. A withholding agent making a payment to such an entity is unlikely to be in a position to determine whether the entity's self-certification regarding its qualification is accurate.

Proposal

Any withholding agent making a payment of U.S.-source FDAP income and gross proceeds from the sale of any property of a type which can produce U.S.-source interest or dividends to a foreign entity (other than a foreign financial institution) would be required to withhold a tax of 30 percent, unless the foreign entity certifies that no U.S. person owns, directly or indirectly, an interest of more than 10 percent or the foreign entity provides the name, address, and TIN of each such substantial U.S. owner, and the withholding agent does not know or have reason to know that any information provided is incorrect. Exceptions would be provided for payments to publicly traded companies and their subsidiaries, foreign governments, international organizations, foreign central banks, any entity that is organized under the laws of a possession of the United States and that is wholly owned by one or more bona fide residents of such possession, and other classes of person identified by the Secretary, or any class of payment identified by the Secretary, as posing a low risk of tax evasion.

The proposal would be effective for payments made after December 31, 2012.

REPEAL CERTAIN FOREIGN EXCEPTIONS TO REGISTERED BOND REQUIREMENTS

Current Law

In general, a taxpayer may deduct all interest paid or accrued within the taxable year on indebtedness. For registration-required obligations, a deduction for interest is allowed only if the obligation is in registered form. Generally, an obligation is treated as issued in registered form if the issuer or its agent maintains a registration of the identity of the owner of the obligation and the obligation can be transferred only through this registration system.

In addition to the denial of an interest deduction, an excise tax is imposed on the issuer of any registration-required obligation that is not in registered form. The excise tax is equal to one percent of the principal amount of the obligation multiplied by the number of calendar years (or portions thereof) during the period beginning on the date of issuance of the obligation and ending on the date of maturity.

Moreover, any gain realized by the beneficial owner of a registration-required obligation that is not in registered form on the sale or other disposition of the obligation is treated as ordinary income (rather than capital gain), unless the issuer of the obligation was subject to the excise tax described above. Finally, deductions for losses realized by beneficial owners of registration-required obligations that are not in registered form are disallowed.

A foreign targeted obligation is excluded from the definition of a registration-required obligation.

Payments of "portfolio interest" are generally exempt from U.S. withholding tax to a nonresident alien or foreign corporation from sources within the United States. Interest on an obligation that is not in registered form may qualify as portfolio interest if the obligation meets the foreign targeting requirements of section 163(f) (2) (B).

Under title 31 of the United States Code, every "registration-required obligation" of the U.S. government must be in registered form, unless it is foreign targeted.

Reasons for Change

Bonds that are not in registered form may allow persons seeking to evade U.S. taxes the ability to invest in such obligations anonymously. Eliminating the foreign-targeted exceptions to the registration requirements will help to ensure that the owners of such obligations are properly identified and that income from such obligations is properly reported.

Proposal

The proposal would repeal the foreign targeted obligation exception to the denial of a deduction for interest on bonds not in registered form. Thus, under the proposal, a deduction for interest would be disallowed with respect to any registration-required obligation not issued in registered form. Under the proposal, a dematerialized book entry system or other book entry system specified by the Secretary would be treated as a book entry system for purposes of determining whether an obligation is in registered form.

Further, under the proposal, the foreign targeted obligation exception would not be available with respect to the ordinary income treatment of any gain realized by the beneficial owner of a registration-required obligation that is not in registered form on the sale or other disposition of the obligation. Similarly, the foreign targeted obligation exception would not be available with respect to the present law rule disallowing deductions for losses realized by a beneficial owner of a registration-required obligation that is not in registered form. The proposal would include a conforming change to title 31 of the United States Code that repeals the foreign targeted exception to the definition of a registration-required obligation.

Finally, under the proposal interest paid on bonds that are not issued in registered form would not be treated as portfolio interest. Under the proposal, interest would qualify as portfolio interest only if it is paid on an obligation that is issued in registered form and for which the beneficial owner has provided the withholding agent with a statement certifying that the beneficial owner is not a United States person, unless the Secretary determines that such a statement is not necessary.

The provision would be effective for obligations issued after the date which is two years after the date of enactment.

REQUIRE DISCLOSURE OF FOREIGN FINANCIAL ASSETS TO BE FILED WITH TAX RETURN

Current Law

United States persons must file certain information reports with respect to certain interests in foreign entities. Upon the formation, acquisition or ongoing ownership of certain foreign corporations, certain U.S. persons must file an information return providing information about foreign corporations in which they hold an interest. Similarly, certain U.S. persons must file information returns with respect to certain interests in a controlled foreign partnership, with respect to certain foreign trusts, and with respect to foreign disregarded entities. In addition, a U.S. person that capitalizes a foreign entity generally must file an information return regarding the transaction.

Under current law, taxpayers generally must indicate on their income tax returns whether they had an interest in or signature or other authority over a financial account in a foreign country during the year to which the tax return relates. If a taxpayer has a foreign account, the tax return refers the taxpayer to the Report of Foreign Bank and Financial Accounts, Form TD F 90-22.1 (FBAR). The FBAR requires the taxpayer to disclose whether, at any time during the preceding year, that person had an interest in, or signature authority over, financial accounts, if the aggregate value of these accounts exceeds $10,000. The FBAR further requires the person to disclose certain information regarding the foreign account, including the account number, financial institution, and maximum value during the year. The FBAR is not required to be filed until June 30 of the year following the calendar year to which it relates. The FBAR is filed with the Treasury Department generally and not directly with the IRS.

Reasons for Change

Disclosure of more detailed information regarding foreign financial assets on the income tax return would assist the IRS in identifying and investigating instances where taxpayers have used foreign financial assets to evade U.S. taxes.

Proposal

Any U.S. individual who holds an interest in a foreign financial account, an interest in a foreign entity or any financial instrument or contract held for investment and issued by a foreign person would be required to file an information return if the aggregate value of all such assets exceeds $50,000. The information return would set forth the name and address of the financial institution that maintains such account or the issuer of the instrument, and the maximum value of the asset during the year. The disclosure would be included as part of the tax return for the taxpayer. Penalties for failing to report the foreign financial asset would be consistent with current penalties under current law for failing to disclose an interest in a foreign entity, such that a failure to report the required information would result in a penalty of $10,000, unless the failure is shown to be due to reasonable cause and not willful neglect. The Secretary would be given regulatory authority to apply the proposal to certain domestic entities formed or availed of for purposes of holding foreign financial assets, and to coordinate the proposal with other information returns required under the Code.

A rebuttable evidentiary presumption would be applicable in a civil administrative or judicial proceeding providing that, if it is established that the individual had an interest in an undisclosed foreign financial asset, then the aggregate value of all foreign financial assets in which a U.S. individual has an interest will be presumed to exceed $50,000. The rebuttable evidentiary presumption would not apply in criminal proceedings.

The tax return disclosure would not replace or mitigate the individual's obligation to separately file an FBAR with the Treasury Department as required under Title 31. The penalties imposed under Title 31 for failing to file an FBAR would continue to apply to a failure to file an FBAR as required under Title 31. Failure to disclose the foreign accounts with the income tax return would not be subject to the Title 31 penalties, although it could give rise to penalties and other consequences imposed under the Code, including extension of the statute of limitations.

The proposal would be effective for taxable years beginning after the date of enactment.

IMPOSE PENALTIES FOR UNDERPAYMENTS ATTRIBUTABLE TO UNDISCLOSED FOREIGN FINANCIAL ASSETS

Current Law

Current law imposes a 20-percent accuracy-related penalty on (i) a substantial understatement of income tax, (ii) an understatement resulting from negligence or disregard of rules or regulations, and (iii) an understatement related to a reportable transaction. The 20-percent accuracy-related penalty increases to 30 percent in the case of an understatement from a reportable transaction that was not properly disclosed. The accuracy-related penalty is not imposed when the taxpayer demonstrates "reasonable cause" for the position and acted in good faith. In the case of a reportable transaction, the reasonable cause exception to the imposition of penalties only applies if the taxpayer disclosed the reportable transaction as required by law and certain other requirements are met.

Individual taxpayers must indicate on their income tax returns whether they had an interest in or signature or other authority over a financial account in a foreign country during the year to which the tax return relates. If the taxpayer had a foreign financial account, the income tax return instructs the taxpayer to refer to the Report of Foreign Bank and Financial Accounts (FBAR), which requires the taxpayer to disclose information regarding certain foreign accounts.

Under present law, failure to comply with the various information reporting requirements generally does not, in itself, determine the amount of the penalty imposed on an underpayment of tax.

Reasons for Change

United States persons may seek to evade U.S. tax liability by holding foreign financial assets. Increasing the penalties on understatements from transactions that involve undisclosed foreign financial assets would encourage proper disclosure of such accounts and deter the use of foreign financial assets to evade U.S. tax liability.

Proposal

In addition to the circumstances identified under current law, the 20-percent accuracy-related penalty would apply to any understatement attributable to undisclosed foreign financial assets. In addition, the proposal would double the 20-percent accuracy-related penalty to 40 percent in the case of such foreign financial asset understatements. Undisclosed foreign financial assets would be foreign financial assets that the taxpayer failed to disclose properly under section 6038, 6038B, 6046A, 6048, or the proposed requirement that taxpayers disclose foreign financial assets. As under current law, the penalty would not be imposed when the understatement is due to reasonable cause.

The proposal would be effective for taxable years beginning after the date of enactment.

EXTEND STATUTE OF LIMITATIONS FOR SIGNIFICANT OMISSION OF INCOME ATTRIBUTABLE TO FOREIGN FINANCIAL ASSETS

Current Law

In general, additional Federal tax liabilities in the form of tax, interest, penalties, and additions to tax must be assessed by the IRS within three years after the date a return is filed. If an assessment is not made within the required time period, the additional liabilities generally cannot be assessed or collected at any future time. Section 6501(c)(8) of the Code provides an exception to this general statute of limitations with respect to any tax relating to any event or period for which certain information returns are required with respect to certain foreign transfers, foreign entities, and foreign-owned entities. In these cases, the statute of limitations does not expire until three years after the taxpayer furnishes the information required to be reported.

Section 6038A of the Code requires certain foreign-owned domestic corporations to file information returns containing specified information with respect to related-party transactions, and to maintain such records as may be appropriate to determine the correct treatment of such transactions. Failure to file the required information returns triggers the section 6501(c)(8) extension of the statute of limitations.

A special rule is provided where there is a substantial omission of income. If a taxpayer omits substantial gross income on a return, any tax with respect to that return may be assessed and collected within six years of the date on which the return was filed. In the case of income taxes, a substantial omission means at least 25 percent of the amount that was properly includible in gross income; for estate and gift taxes, a substantial omission means 25 percent of a gross estate or total gifts.

Reasons for Change

Compliance with reporting and recordkeeping obligations is essential in order to enable the IRS to enforce the tax laws. The three-year period provided by section 6501(c)(8) does not always allow sufficient time for the IRS to determine a taxpayer's tax liability where the taxpayer has omitted income and failed to disclose foreign assets.

Proposal

Under the proposal, if the taxpayer omits from gross income more than $5,000 that is attributable to one or more foreign financial assets required to be disclosed under the proposal to require disclosure of foreign financial assets (without regard to the $50,000 threshold), the statute of limitation would be extended to six years after the required return was filed. In addition, the tolling of the statute of limitations under section 6501(c)(8) would apply to failures to file the reports that would be required under the proposal to require reporting of foreign financial assets.

The proposal would be effective for income tax returns due to be filed after the date of enactment, and returns filed on or before such date if the statute of limitations with respect to such return has not expired as of the date of enactment.

REQUIRE REPORTING OF CERTAIN TRANSFERS OF ASSETS TO OR FROM FOREIGN FINANCIAL ACCOUNTS

Current Law

United States persons must disclose whether, at any time during the preceding year, they had an interest in, or signature or other authority over, financial accounts in a foreign country, if the aggregate value of these accounts exceeds $10,000. United States persons must also report certain information with respect to certain foreign business entities that they control. Under Treasury regulations, a U.S. person controls a foreign corporation for this purpose if the person owns, actually or constructively, more than 50 percent of the corporation's stock, by vote or by value. Current law does not contain a provision that generally requires reporting of transfers of money or property to, or receipt of money or property from, a foreign bank, brokerage, or other financial account by U.S. individuals.

Reasons for Change

The Administration is concerned about the use of foreign accounts by U.S. citizens and residents to evade U.S. tax. To reduce such evasion, the Administration proposes to increase information reporting requirements with respect to transfers to and from certain foreign accounts.

Proposal

A U.S. individual would be required to report, on the individual's income tax return, any transfer of money or property made to, or receipt of money or property from, any foreign bank, brokerage, or other financial account by the individual. Additionally, any entity of which a U.S. individual owns, directly or indirectly, more than 25 percent of the ownership interest would be required to report any transfer of money or property made to, or receipt of money or property from, any foreign bank, brokerage, or other financial account by the entity. Such an entity would also be required to report the name, address, and taxpayer identification number of any U.S. individual who owns more than 25 percent of the ownership interest in the entity. This reporting requirement would not apply if the cumulative amount or value of transfers, and the cumulative amount or value of receipts that would otherwise be reportable for a given year were each less than $50,000. The Treasury Department would receive regulatory authority to require the reporting of additional information, including classifying transfers and receipts as for investment or for arm's-length payments in the ordinary course of business for services or tangible property, or such other categories as the Secretary may prescribe. Failure to report a covered transfer would result in the imposition of a penalty equal to the lesser of $10,000 per reportable transfer or 10 percent of the cumulative amount or value of the unreported covered transfers. No penalty would be imposed for a failure to report due to reasonable cause. The Treasury Department would receive regulatory authority to issue rules to prevent abuse of the reporting exemptions and to provide exceptions to the reporting requirement.

The proposal would be effective for transfers made after December 31, 2012.

REQUIRE THIRD-PARTY INFORMATION REPORTING REGARDING THE TRANSFER OF ASSETS TO OR FROM FOREIGN FINANCIAL ACCOUNTS AND THE ESTABLISHMENT OF FOREIGN FINANCIAL ACCOUNTS

Current Law

United States persons must disclose whether, at any time during the preceding year, they had an interest in, or signature or other authority over, financial accounts in a foreign country, if the aggregate value of these accounts exceeds $10,000. Current law does not generally require third-party information reporting to the IRS with regard to the transfer of money or property to, or receipt of money or property from, a foreign bank, brokerage, or other financial account on behalf of a U.S. person, or with regard to the establishment of a foreign bank, brokerage, or other financial account on behalf of a U.S. person.

Reasons for Change

The Administration is concerned that U.S. persons are failing to comply with the requirement to report certain foreign financial accounts. Establishing a third-party reporting requirement with respect to transfers to foreign financial accounts, receipts from such accounts, and the establishment of such accounts would lead to greater disclosure of foreign financial accounts, and consequently would discourage the evasion of U.S. taxation. These third-party reporting requirements complement taxpayer reporting requirements.

Proposal

Any U.S. financial institution that during the year transfers to, or receives from, a foreign bank, brokerage, or other financial account money or property with an aggregate value of more than $50,000 on behalf of a U.S. individual, or on behalf of any entity of which a U.S. individual owns, directly or indirectly, more than 25 percent of the ownership interest, would be required to file an information return regarding such transfer or receipt (including, in the case of a transfer by an entity, the name, address, and taxpayer identification number (TIN) of any U.S. individual who owns more than 25 percent of the ownership interest in such entity). Any U.S. financial institution that opens a foreign bank, brokerage, or other financial account on behalf of a U.S. individual, or on behalf of any entity of which a U.S. individual owns, directly or indirectly, more than 25 percent of the ownership interest, would be required to file an information return with the IRS regarding such account, including reporting any amounts of money or property transferred by the financial institution to, or received by it from, such account.

In addition to filing an information return with the Internal Revenue Service, the U.S. financial institution would be required to send a copy of such return to the U.S. individual, or entity, as to which the return is made.

Reporting would not be required where the U.S. financial institution determined the entity making or receiving the transfer was: a publicly traded corporation, or a subsidiary thereof; an organization exempt from tax under section 501; an individual retirement plan; the United States or any wholly owned agency or instrumentality thereof; any State, the District of Columbia, any possession of the United States, any political subdivision of any of the foregoing, or any wholly owned agency or instrumentality of any one or more of the foregoing; any bank (as defined in section 581); any real estate investment trust (as defined in section 856); any regulated investment company (as defined in section 851); any common trust fund (as defined in section 584(a)); any trust which is exempt from tax under section 664(c) or is described in section 4947(a)(1); or an entity engaged in an active trade or business (other than the business of investing or similar activities).

Failure to file a required information return or to provide a copy of such return to the U.S. individual would result in the imposition of a penalty of $50 with respect to each such failure. In the case of a failure to file due to intentional disregard, the penalty would be the greater of $100 or 5 percent of the amount of the items required to be reported. No penalty would be imposed for a failure to report due to reasonable cause.

The Treasury Department would receive regulatory authority to provide additional exceptions (including where the Secretary determines that the reporting would be duplicative of other reporting requirements), to limit the types of transfers subject to the reporting requirement, to require that certain additional information be reported, and to permit U.S. financial institutions to report additional transfers of money or property to, or from, a foreign bank, brokerage, or other financial account on behalf of a U.S. individual (or on behalf of an entity of which the U.S. individual owns, actually or constructively, more than 25 percent of the ownership interest).

The proposal would be effective for amounts transferred and accounts opened beginning after December 31, 2012.

PERMIT THE SECRETARY TO REQUIRE ELECTRONIC FILING BY FINANCIAL INSTITUTIONS OF CERTAIN WITHHOLDING TAX RETURNS

Current Law

Every withholding agent must file an annual return with the IRS on Form 1042, reporting all taxes withheld during the preceding year and remitting taxes still owing for such preceding year. A withholding agent also must file an information return on Form 1042-S, providing all items of income specified in section 1441(b) paid during the previous year to foreign persons.

Reasons for Change

The Secretary's authority to require returns electronically is limited to persons required to file at least 250 returns during the year. Electronic filing reduces errors on the required returns and facilitates compliance and enforcement measures by the IRS.

Proposal

The proposal would permit the Treasury Department to issue regulations requiring electronic filing for any return filed by a financial institution with respect to any taxes withheld by the financial institution, regardless of the general 250 return threshold.

The proposal would apply to returns the due date for which (determined without regard to extensions) is after the date of enactment.

ESTABLISH PRESUMPTION OF U.S. BENEFICIARY IN CASE OF TRANSFERS TO FOREIGN TRUSTS BY A U.S. PERSON

Current Law

A U.S. person that directly or indirectly transfers property to a foreign trust is generally treated as the owner of the portion of the trust attributable to that property for any year in which there is a U.S. beneficiary of any portion of the trust. A trust is treated as having a U.S. beneficiary for a taxable year unless under the terms of the trust, no part of the income or corpus of the trust may be paid or accumulated during the taxable year to or for the benefit of any U.S. person, and if the trust were terminated at any time during the taxable year, no part of the income or corpus of the trust could be paid to or for the benefit of a U.S. person.

Reasons for Change

In the absence of adequate information reporting, it is difficult for the IRS to determine whether a trust has a U.S. beneficiary. A presumption that a foreign trust receiving a transfer of property from a U.S. person has a U.S. beneficiary unless the transferor provides sufficient information with respect to the existence of U.S. beneficiaries will improve the ability of the IRS to enforce U.S. tax rules applicable to foreign trusts.

Proposal

Under the proposal, if a U.S. person directly or indirectly transfers property to a foreign trust (other than certain deferred compensation and charitable trusts), the trust would be presumed to have a U.S. beneficiary for purposes of the grantor trust rules unless the U.S. transferor files an information return with the IRS and demonstrates that (1) under the terms of the trust, no part of the income or corpus of the trust may be paid or accumulated during the taxable year to or for the benefit of any U.S. person, and (2) if the trust were terminated at any time during the taxable year, no part of the income or corpus of the trust could be paid to or for the benefit of any U.S. person. The proposal would also make certain clarifications of existing rules applicable to foreign trusts with U.S. grantors and beneficiaries.

This proposal would be effective for transfers of property made after the date of enactment.

TREAT CERTAIN UNCOMPENSATED USES OF FOREIGN TRUST PROPERTY AS A DISTRIBUTION TO U.S. GRANTOR OR BENEFICIARY

Current Law

In general, if a foreign trust makes a loan of cash or marketable securities directly or indirectly to any grantor or beneficiary of the trust who is a U.S. person, or to any U.S. person related to such grantor or beneficiary, the amount of the loan is treated as a distribution by the foreign trust to the grantor or beneficiary. In addition, the trust is not treated as a simple trust for the year of the distribution. The grantor trust rules do not currently treat a U.S. person receiving an uncompensated loan of cash or marketable securities, or the uncompensated use of trust property, as a U.S. beneficiary.

Reasons for Change

The administration is concerned that foreign trusts may permit the uncompensated use of trust property by U.S. persons without treating the value of the use as a trust distribution, and without treating the recipient as a U.S. beneficiary for purposes of the grantor trust rules.

Proposal

Under the proposal, if a foreign trust permits the use of trust property other than cash or marketable securities by a U.S. grantor or beneficiary (or a related U.S. person), the fair market value of the use of such property would be treated as a distribution to the U.S. grantor or beneficiary, except to the extent that the trust is paid the fair market value of such use within a reasonable period of time. In addition, for purposes of the grantor trust rules, a loan of cash or marketable securities or the use of other property of a foreign trust would be treated as paid or accumulated for the benefit of a U.S. person, except to the extent that the U.S. person repays the loan at market rates (or pays the fair market value of the use) within a reasonable period of time.

This proposal would be effective for loans made, and uses of property, after the date of enactment.

IMPROVE FOREIGN TRUST REPORTING PENALTY

Current Law

Certain information must be reported to the IRS with respect to certain foreign trusts. A civil penalty applies to persons who fail to file a timely return as required or who file an incomplete or incorrect return. Generally, the penalty is equal to 35 percent of the "gross reportable amount," which is defined as the gross value of property involved in a reportable event such as a gratuitous transfer to the trust, the gross value of the portion of the trust's assets at the close of the year that is treated as owned by a United States person, or the gross amount of distributions received from the trust. In the case of a failure to report that continues for more than 90 days after the IRS mails notice of such failure, the penalty (in addition to the 35 percent penalty) is $10,000 for each 30-day period (or fraction thereof) during which the failure continues. The total penalty with respect to any failure may not exceed the gross reportable amount.

Reasons for Change

In many instances, the IRS obtains information relating to the creation of a foreign trust from third parties, or the IRS discovers funding of a foreign trust from public records. Without the cooperation of persons actually involved with the trust, however, it is often difficult for the IRS to determine the gross reportable amount. If the IRS cannot determine the gross reportable amount, the IRS may not be able to assess the penalties, including the $10,000 penalty for continued failure to report. The current penalty regime therefore may create an incentive for persons subject to the reporting requirement not to report or cooperate with the IRS in the hope that the IRS will not be able to determine the gross reportable amount, which is essential to presenting a prima facie case sufficient to meet the Code section 7491(c) burden of production to support the penalty.

Proposal

The penalty provision would be amended to impose an initial penalty of the greater of $10,000 or 35 percent of the gross reportable amount (if the gross reportable amount is known). The additional $10,000 penalty for continued failure to report would remain unchanged. Thus, even if the gross reportable amount is not known, the IRS may impose a $10,000 penalty on a person who fails to report timely or correctly as required, and may impose a $10,000 penalty for each 30-day period (or fraction thereof) that the failure to report continues. If the person subsequently provides enough information for the IRS to determine the gross reportable amount, the total penalties would be capped at that amount and any excess penalty already paid would be refunded. Accordingly, a person can stop the compounding of penalties by cooperating with the IRS so that it can determine the gross reportable amount.

The proposal would be effective for information reports required to be filed after December 31 of the year of enactment.

Reform Treatment of Insurance Companies and Products

MODIFY RULES THAT APPLY TO SALES OF LIFE INSURANCE CONTRACTS

Current Law

The seller of a life insurance contract generally must report as taxable income the difference between the amount received from the buyer and the adjusted basis in the contract, unless the buyer is a viatical settlement provider and the insured person is terminally or chronically ill.

Under a transfer-for-value rule, the buyer of a previously-issued life insurance contract who subsequently receives a death benefit generally is subject to tax on the difference between the death benefit received and the sum of the amount paid for the contract and premiums subsequently paid by the buyer. This rule does not apply if the buyer's basis is determined in whole or in part by reference to the seller's basis, nor does the rule apply if the buyer is the insured, a partner of the insured, a partnership in which the insured is a partner, or a corporation in which the insured is a shareholder or officer.

Persons engaged in a trade or business that make payments of premiums, compensations, remunerations, other fixed or determinable gains, profits and income, or certain other types of payments in the course of that trade or business to another person generally are required to report such payments of $600 or more to the IRS. However, reporting may not be required in some circumstances involving the purchase of a life insurance contract.

Reasons for Change

Recent years have seen a significant increase in the number and size of life settlement transactions, wherein individuals sell previously-issued life insurance contracts to investors. Compliance is sometimes hampered by a lack of information reporting. In addition, the current law exceptions to the transfer-for-value rule may give investors the ability to structure a transaction to avoid paying tax on the profit when the insured person dies.

Proposal

The proposal would require a person or entity who purchases an interest in an existing life insurance contract with a death benefit equal to or exceeding $500,000 to report the purchase price, the buyer's and seller's taxpayer identification numbers (TINs), and the issuer and policy number to the IRS, to the insurance company that issued the policy, and to the seller.

The proposal also would modify the transfer-for-value rule to ensure that exceptions to that rule would not apply to buyers of policies. Upon the payment of any policy benefits to the buyer, the insurance company would be required to report the gross benefit payment, the buyer's TIN, and the insurance company's estimate of the buyer's basis to the IRS and to the payee.

The proposal would apply to sales or assignment of interests in life insurance policies and payments of death benefits for taxable years beginning after December 31, 2010.

MODIFY DIVIDENDS-RECEIVED DEDUCTION FOR LIFE INSURANCE COMPANY SEPARATE ACCOUNTS

Current Law

Corporate taxpayers may generally qualify for a dividends-received deduction (DRD) with regard to dividends received from other domestic corporations, in order to prevent or limit taxable inclusion of the same income by more than one corporation. No DRD is allowed, however, in respect of any dividend on any share of stock (1) to the extent the taxpayer is under an obligation to make related payments with respect to positions in substantially similar or related property, or (2) that is held by the taxpayer for 45 days or less during the 91-day period beginning on the date that is 45 days before the share becomes ex-dividend with respect to the dividend. For this purpose, the taxpayer's holding period is reduced for any period in which the taxpayer has diminished its risk of loss by holding one or more positions with respect to substantially similar or related property.

In the case of a life insurance company, the DRD is permitted only with regard to the "company's share" of dividends received, reflecting the fact that some portion of the company's dividend income is used to fund tax-deductible reserves for its obligations to policyholders. Likewise, the net increase or net decrease in reserves is computed by reducing the ending balance of the reserve items by the policyholders' share of tax-exempt interest. The regime for computing the company's share and policyholders' share of net investment income is sometimes referred to as proration.

A life insurance company's separate account assets, liabilities, and income are segregated from those of the company's general account in order to support variable life insurance and variable annuity contracts. A company's share and policyholders' share are computed for the company's general account and separately for each separate account.

The policyholders' share equals 100 percent less the company's share, whereas the latter is equal to the company's share of net investment income divided by net investment income. The company's share of net investment income is the excess, if any, of net investment income over certain amounts, including "required interest," that are set aside to satisfy obligations to policyholders. Required interest with regard to an account is calculated by multiplying a specified account earnings rate by the mean of the reserves with regard to the account for the taxable year.

Reasons for Change

The proration methodology currently used by some taxpayers may produce a company's share that greatly exceeds the company's economic interest in the net investment income earned by its separate account assets, generating controversy between life insurance companies and the IRS. The purposes of the proration regime would be better served, and life insurance companies would be treated more like other taxpayers with a diminished risk of loss in stock or an obligation to make related payments with respect to dividends, if the company's share bore a more direct relationship to the company's actual economic interest in the account.

Proposal

As under current law, required interest under the proposal would equal an earnings rate times the mean of reserves. For a separate account, the earnings rate would equal a gross earnings rate (net investment income of the account, divided by the mean of the account's assets), minus a company-retained percentage (amounts retained by the company from the account's net investment income, if any, divided by the mean of reserves). For this purpose, amounts retained by the company would be treated as funded proportionately by items included in net investment income and items not so included. Under the proposal, the company's share with regard to a separate account would approximate the ratio of the mean of the surplus attributable to the account to the mean of the account's assets. The company's share with regard to a company's general account would be computed as under current law.

The proposal would be effective for taxable years beginning after December 31, 2010.

EXPAND PRO RATA INTEREST EXPENSE DISALLOWANCE FOR CORPORATE-OWNED LIFE INSURANCE (COLI)

Current Law

In general, no Federal income tax is imposed on a policyholder with respect to the earnings credited under a life insurance or endowment contract, and Federal income tax generally is deferred with respect to earnings under an annuity contract (unless the annuity contract is owned by a person other than a natural person). In addition, amounts received under a life insurance contract by reason of the death of the insured generally are excluded from gross income of the recipient.

Interest on policy loans or other indebtedness with respect to life insurance, endowment or annuity contracts generally is not deductible, unless the insurance contract insures the life of a key person of the business. A key person includes a 20-percent owner of the business, as well as a limited number of the business' officers or employees. However, this interest disallowance rule applies to businesses only to the extent that the indebtedness can be traced to a life insurance, endowment or annuity contract.

In addition, the interest deductions of a business other than an insurance company are reduced to the extent the interest is allocable to unborrowed policy cash values based on a statutory formula. An exception to the pro rata interest disallowance applies with respect to contracts that cover individuals who are officers, directors, employees, or 20-percent owners of the taxpayer. In the case of both life and non-life insurance companies, special proration rules similarly require adjustments to prevent or limit the funding of tax-deductible reserve increases with tax preferred income, including earnings credited under life insurance, endowment and annuity contracts that would be subject to the pro rata interest disallowance rule if owned by a non-insurance company.

Reasons for Change

Leveraged businesses can fund deductible interest expenses with tax-exempt or tax-deferred income credited under life insurance, endowment or annuity contracts insuring certain types of individuals. For example, these businesses frequently invest in investment-oriented insurance policies covering the lives of their employees, officers, directors or owners. These entities generally do not take out policy loans or other indebtedness that is secured or otherwise traceable to the insurance contracts. Instead, they borrow from depositors or other lenders, or issue bonds. Similar tax arbitrage benefits result when insurance companies invest in certain insurance contracts that cover the lives of their employees, officers, directors or 20-percent shareholders and fund deductible reserves with tax-exempt or tax-deferred income.

Proposal

The proposal would repeal the exception from the pro rata interest expense disallowance rule for contracts covering employees, officers or directors, other than 20-percent owners of a business that is the owner or beneficiary of the contracts.

The proposal would apply to contracts issued after December 31, 2010, in taxable years ending after that date. For this purpose, any material increase in the death benefit or other material change in the contract would be treated as a new contract except that in the case of a master contract, the addition of covered lives would be treated as a new contract only with respect to the additional covered lives.

PERMIT PARTIAL ANNUITIZATION OF A NONQUALIFIED ANNUITY CONTRACT

Current Law

If a taxpayer receives an amount as an annuity under a nonqualified, deferred annuity contract, a proportionate part of the amount received is excluded from gross income because it is considered to represent a return of premiums or other consideration paid for the annuity. The proportionate part that is excluded from gross income is determined by an exclusion ratio, which equals the investment in the contract as of the annuity starting date divided by the expected return under the contract as of that date.

If, on the other hand, an amount is received under an annuity contract but not as an annuity, the amount either is included in gross income (if received on or after the annuity starting date) or is included in gross income to the extent allocable to income on the contract (if received before the annuity starting date).

The annuity starting date is the first day of the first period for which an amount is received as an annuity. This date is generally the later of the date on which the obligations under the contract became fixed, or the first day of the period that ends on the date of the first annuity payment.

Reasons for Change

Under current law, a taxpayer may exchange a portion of an existing annuity contract for a second annuity contract and, under certain circumstances, annuitize one of the contracts involved in the exchange. An exclusion ratio then applies to determine the extent to which amounts received as an annuity under the annuitized contracts are included in gross income. Current law does not, however, address the treatment of a transaction (sometimes known as a partial annuitization) in which the holder of an annuity contract irrevocably elects to apply only a portion of the contract to purchase a stream of annuity payments under the contract, leaving the remainder of the contract to accumulate income on a tax-deferred basis. It is appropriate that these transactions be treated consistently.

Moreover, the possibility that a partial annuitization could be taxed on an income-first basis rather than on a proportionate basis discourages some taxpayers from annuitizing existing deferred annuity contracts at a time when annuity payments are needed to fund their retirement.

Proposal

An exclusion ratio would apply to each amount received as an annuity with regard to a portion of a nonqualified deferred annuity contract that is partially annuitized. This treatment would be available only if: (1) the taxpayer irrevocably elects to apply a portion of the contract to purchase a stream of annuity payments; (2) the stream of annuity payments is either for at least ten years or for the life of one or more individuals; and (3) the exclusion ratio is computed based on the expected return and investment in the contract with regard to the portion of the contract that is annuitized.

The proposal would be effective for partial annuitizations that are effected after December 31, 2010.

ELIMINATE FOSSIL FUEL TAX PREFERENCES

Eliminate Oil and Gas Company Preferences

REPEAL ENHANCED OIL RECOVERY CREDIT

Current Law

The general business credit includes a 15-percent credit for eligible costs attributable to enhanced oil recovery (EOR) projects. If the credit is claimed with respect to eligible costs, the taxpayer's deduction (or basis increase) with respect to those costs is reduced by the amount of the credit. Eligible costs include the cost of constructing a gas treatment plant to prepare Alaska natural gas for pipeline transportation and any of the following costs with respect to a qualified EOR project: (1) the cost of depreciable or amortizable tangible property that is an integral part of the project; (2) intangible drilling and development costs (IDCs) that the taxpayer can elect to deduct; and (3) deductible tertiary injectant costs. A qualified EOR project must be located in the United States and must involve the application of one or more of nine listed tertiary recovery methods that can reasonably be expected to result in more than an insignificant increase in the amount of crude oil which ultimately will be recovered. The allowable credit is phased out over a $6 range for a taxable year if the annual average unregulated wellhead price per barrel of domestic crude oil during the calendar year preceding the calendar year in which the taxable year begins (the reference price) exceeds an inflation adjusted threshold. The credit was completely phased out for taxable years beginning in 2009, because the reference price ($94.03) exceeded the inflation adjusted threshold ($42.01) by more than $6.

Reasons for Change

The President agreed at the G-20 Summit in Pittsburgh to phase out subsidies for fossil fuels so that the United States can transition to a 21st century energy economy. The credit, like other oil and gas preferences the Administration proposes to repeal, distorts markets by encouraging more investment in the oil and gas industry than would occur under a neutral system. To the extent the credit encourages overproduction of oil, it is detrimental to long-term energy security and is also inconsistent with the Administration's policy of reducing carbon emissions and encouraging the use of renewable energy sources. Moreover, the credit must ultimately be financed with taxes that result in underinvestment in other, potentially more productive, areas of the economy.

Proposal

The investment tax credit for enhanced oil recovery projects would be repealed for taxable years beginning after December 31, 2010.

REPEAL CREDIT FOR OIL AND GAS PRODUCED FROM MARGINAL WELLS

Current Law

The general business credit includes a credit for crude oil and natural gas produced from marginal wells. The credit rate is $3.00 per barrel of oil and $0.50 per 1,000 cubic feet of natural gas for taxable years beginning in 2005 and is adjusted for inflation in taxable years beginning after 2005. The credit is available for production from wells that produce oil and gas qualifying as marginal production for purposes of the percentage depletion rules or that have average daily production of not more than 25 barrel-of-oil equivalents and produce at least 95 percent water. The credit per well is limited to 1,095 barrels of oil or barrel-of-oil equivalents per year. The credit rate for crude oil is phased out for a taxable year if the annual average unregulated wellhead price per barrel of domestic crude oil during the calendar year preceding the calendar year in which the taxable year begins (the reference price) exceeds the applicable threshold. The phase-out range and the applicable threshold at which phase-out begins are $3.00 and $15.00 for taxable years beginning in 2005 and are adjusted for inflation in taxable years beginning after 2005. The credit rate for natural gas is similarly phased out for a taxable year if the annual average wellhead price for domestic natural gas exceeds the applicable threshold. The phase-out range and the applicable threshold at which phase-out begins are $0.33 and $1.67 for taxable years beginning in 2005 and are adjusted for inflation in taxable years beginning after 2005. The credit has been completely phased out for all taxable years since its enactment. The marginal well credit can be carried back up to five years unlike other components of the general business credit, which can be carried back only one year.

Reasons for Change

The President agreed at the G-20 Summit in Pittsburgh to phase out subsidies for fossil fuels so that the United States can transition to a 21st century energy economy. The credit, like other oil and gas preferences the Administration proposes to repeal, distorts markets by encouraging more investment in the oil and gas industry than would occur under a neutral system. To the extent the credit encourages overproduction of oil, it is detrimental to long-term energy security and is also inconsistent with the Administration's policy of reducing carbon emissions and encouraging the use of renewable energy sources. Moreover, the credit must ultimately be financed with taxes that result in underinvestment in other, potentially more productive, areas of the economy.

Proposal

The production tax credit for oil and gas from marginal wells would be repealed for production in taxable years beginning after December 31, 2010.

REPEAL EXPENSING OF INTANGIBLE DRILLING COSTS

Current Law

In general, costs that benefit future periods must be capitalized and recovered over such periods for income tax purposes, rather than being expensed in the period the costs are incurred. In addition, the uniform capitalization rules require certain direct and indirect costs allocable to property to be included in inventory or capitalized as part of the basis of such property. In general, the uniform capitalization rules apply to real and tangible personal property produced by the taxpayer or acquired for resale.

Special rules apply to intangible drilling and development costs (IDCs). IDCs include all expenditures made by an operator for wages, fuel, repairs, hauling, supplies, and other expenses incident to and necessary for the drilling of wells and the preparation of wells for the production of oil and gas. In addition, IDCs include the cost to operators of any drilling or development work (excluding amounts payable only out of production or gross or net proceeds from production, if the amounts are depletable income to the recipient, and amounts properly allocable to the cost of depreciable property) done by contractors under any form of contract (including a turnkey contract). IDCs include amounts paid for labor, fuel, repairs, hauling, and supplies which are used in the drilling, shooting, and cleaning of wells; in such clearing of ground, draining, road making, surveying, and geological works as are necessary in preparation for the drilling of wells; and in the construction of such derricks, tanks, pipelines, and other physical structures as are necessary for the drilling of wells and the preparation of wells for the production of oil and gas. Generally, IDCs do not include expenses for items which have a salvage value (such as pipes and casings) or items which are part of the acquisition price of an interest in the property.

Under the special rules applicable to IDCs, an operator (i.e., a person who holds a working or operating interest in any tract or parcel of land either as a fee owner or under a lease or any other form of contract granting working or operating rights) who pays or incurs IDCs in the development of an oil or gas property located in the United States may elect either to expense or capitalize those costs. The uniform capitalization rules do not apply to otherwise deductible IDCs.

If a taxpayer elects to expense IDCs, the amount of the IDCs is deductible as an expense in the taxable year the cost is paid or incurred. Generally, IDCs that a taxpayer elects to capitalize may be recovered through depletion or depreciation, as appropriate; or in the case of a nonproductive well ("dry hole"), the operator may elect to deduct the costs. In the case of an integrated oil company (i.e., a company that engages, either directly or through a related enterprise, in substantial retailing or refining activities) that has elected to expense IDCs, 30 percent of the IDCs on productive wells must be capitalized and amortized over a 60-month period.

A taxpayer that has elected to deduct IDCs may, nevertheless, elect to capitalize and amortize certain IDCs over a 60-month period beginning with the month the expenditure was paid or incurred. This rule applies on an expenditure-by-expenditure basis; that is, for any particular taxable year, a taxpayer may deduct some portion of its IDCs and capitalize the rest under this provision. This allows the taxpayer to reduce or eliminate IDC adjustments or preferences under the alternative minimum tax.

The election to deduct IDCs applies only to those IDCs associated with domestic properties. For this purpose, the United States includes certain wells drilled offshore.

Reasons for Change

The President agreed at the G-20 Summit in Pittsburgh to phase out subsidies for fossil fuels so that the United States can transition to a 21st century energy economy. The expensing of IDCs, like other oil and gas preferences the Administration proposes to repeal, distorts markets by encouraging more investment in the oil and gas industry than would occur under a neutral system. To the extent expensing encourages overproduction of oil and gas, it is detrimental to long-term energy security and is also inconsistent with the Administration's policy of reducing carbon emissions and encouraging the use of renewable energy sources. Moreover, the tax subsidy for oil and gas must ultimately be financed with taxes that result in underinvestment in other, potentially more productive, areas of the economy. Capitalization of IDCs would place the oil and gas industry on a cost recovery system similar to that employed by other industries and reduce economic distortions.

Proposal

Expensing of intangible drilling costs and 60-month amortization of capitalized intangible drilling costs would not be allowed. Intangible drilling costs would be capitalized as depreciable or depletable property, depending on the nature of the cost incurred, in accordance with the generally applicable rules.

The proposal would be effective for costs paid or incurred after December 31, 2010.

REPEAL DEDUCTION FOR TERTIARY INJECTANTS

Current Law

Taxpayers are allowed to deduct the cost of qualified tertiary injectant expenses for the taxable year. Qualified tertiary injectant expenses are amounts paid or incurred for any tertiary injectants (other than recoverable hydrocarbon injectants) that are used as a part of a tertiary recovery method. The deduction is treated as an amortization deduction in determining the amount subject to recapture upon disposition of the property.

Reasons for Change

The President agreed at the G-20 Summit in Pittsburgh to phase out subsidies for fossil fuels so that the United States can transition to a 21st century energy economy. The deduction for tertiary injectants, like other oil and gas preferences the Administration proposes to repeal, distorts markets by encouraging more investment in the oil and gas industry than would occur under a neutral system. To the extent expensing encourages overproduction of oil and gas, it is detrimental to long-term energy security and is also inconsistent with the Administration's policy of reducing carbon emissions and encouraging the use of renewable energy sources. Moreover, the tax subsidy for oil and gas must ultimately be financed with taxes that result in underinvestment in other, potentially more productive, areas of the economy. Capitalization of tertiary injectants would place the oil and gas industry on a cost recovery system similar to that employed by other industries and reduce economic distortions.

Proposal

The deduction for qualified tertiary injectant expenses would not be allowed for amounts paid or incurred after December 31, 2010.

REPEAL EXEMPTION TO PASSIVE LOSS LIMITATION FOR WORKING INTERESTS IN OIL AND GAS PROPERTIES

Current Law

The passive loss rules limit deductions and credits from passive trade or business activities. Deductions attributable to passive activities, to the extent they exceed income from passive activities, generally may not be deducted against other income, such as wages, portfolio income, or business income that is not derived from a passive activity. A similar rule applies to credits. Suspended deductions and credits are carried forward and treated as deductions and credits from passive activities in the next year. The suspended losses and credits from a passive activity are allowed in full when the taxpayer completely disposes of the activity.

Passive activities are defined to include trade or business activities in which the taxpayer does not materially participate. An exception is provided, however, for any working interest in an oil or gas property that the taxpayer holds directly or through an entity that does not limit the liability of the taxpayer with respect to the interest.

Reasons for Change

The President agreed at the G-20 Summit in Pittsburgh to phase out subsidies for fossil fuels so that the United States can transition to a 21st century energy economy. The special tax treatment of working interests in oil and gas properties, like other oil and gas preferences the Administration proposes to repeal, distorts markets by encouraging more investment in the oil and gas industry than would occur under a neutral system. To the extent this special treatment encourages overproduction of oil and gas, it is detrimental to long-term energy security and is also inconsistent with the Administration's policy of reducing carbon emissions and encouraging the use of renewable energy sources. Moreover, the working interest exception for oil and gas must ultimately be financed with taxes that result in underinvestment in other, potentially more productive, areas of the economy. Eliminating the working interest exception would subject oil and gas properties to the same limitations as other activities and reduce economic distortions.

Proposal

The exception from the passive loss rules for working interests in oil and gas properties would be repealed for taxable years beginning after December 31, 2010.

REPEAL PERCENTAGE DEPLETION FOR OIL AND NATURAL GAS WELLS

Current Law

The capital costs of oil and gas wells are recovered through the depletion deduction. Under the cost depletion method, the basis recovery for a taxable year is proportional to the exhaustion of the property during the year. This method does not permit cost recovery deductions that exceed basis or that are allowable on an accelerated basis.

A taxpayer may also qualify for percentage depletion with respect to oil and gas properties. The amount of the deduction is a statutory percentage of the gross income from the property. For oil and gas properties, the percentage ranges from 15 to 25 percent and the deduction may not exceed 100 percent of the taxable income from the property. In addition, the percentage depletion deduction for oil and gas properties may not exceed 65 percent of the taxpayer's overall taxable income (determined before the deduction and with certain other adjustments).

Other limitations and special rules apply to the percentage depletion deduction for oil and gas properties. In general, only independent producers and royalty owners (in contrast to integrated oil companies) qualify for the percentage depletion deduction. In addition, oil and gas producers may claim percentage depletion only with respect to up to 1,000 barrels of average daily production of domestic crude oil or an equivalent amount of domestic natural gas (applied on a combined basis in the case of taxpayers that produce both). This quantity limitation is allocated, at the taxpayer's election, between oil production and gas production and then further allocated within each class among the taxpayer's properties. Special rules apply to oil and gas production from marginal wells (generally, wells for which the average daily production is less than 15 barrels of oil or barrel-of-oil equivalents or that produce only heavy oil). Only marginal well production can qualify for percentage depletion at a rate of more than 15 percent. The rate is increased in a taxable year that begins in a calendar year following a calendar year during which the annual average unregulated wellhead price per barrel of domestic crude oil is less than $20. The increase is one percentage point for each whole dollar of difference between the two amounts. In addition, marginal wells are exempt from the 100-percent-of-net-income limitation described above in taxable years beginning during the period 1998-2007 and in taxable years beginning in 2009. Unless the taxpayer elects otherwise, marginal well production is given priority over other production in applying the 1,000-barrel limitation on percentage depletion.

A qualifying taxpayer determines the depletion deduction for each oil and gas property under both the percentage depletion method and the cost depletion method and deducts the larger of the two amounts. Because percentage depletion is computed without regard to the taxpayer's basis in the depletable property, a taxpayer may continue to claim percentage depletion after all the expenditures incurred to acquire and develop the property have been recovered.

Reasons for Change

The President agreed at the G-20 Summit in Pittsburgh to phase out subsidies for fossil fuels so that the United States can transition to a 21st century energy economy. Percentage depletion effectively provides a lower rate of tax with respect to a favored source of income. The lower rate of tax, like other oil and gas preferences the Administration proposes to repeal, distorts markets by encouraging more investment in the oil and gas industry than would occur under a neutral system. To the extent the lower tax rate encourages overproduction of oil and gas, it is detrimental to long-term energy security and is also inconsistent with the Administration's policy of reducing carbon emissions and encouraging the use of renewable energy sources. Moreover, the tax subsidy for oil and gas must ultimately be financed with taxes that result in underinvestment in other, potentially more productive, areas of the economy.

Cost depletion computed by reference to the taxpayer's basis in the property is the equivalent of economic depreciation. Limiting oil and gas producers to cost depletion would place them on a cost recovery system similar to that employed by other industries and reduce economic distortions.

Proposal

Percentage depletion would not be allowed with respect to oil and gas wells. Taxpayers would be permitted to claim cost depletion on their adjusted basis, if any, in oil and gas wells.

The proposal would be effective for taxable years beginning after December 31, 2010.

REPEAL DOMESTIC MANUFACTURING DEDUCTION FOR OIL AND GAS PRODUCTION

Current Law

A deduction is allowed with respect to income attributable to domestic production activities (the manufacturing deduction). For taxable years beginning after 2009, the manufacturing deduction is generally equal to 9 percent of the lesser of qualified production activities income for the taxable year or taxable income for the taxable year, limited to 50 percent of the W-2 wages of the taxpayer for the taxable year. The deduction for income from oil and gas production activities is computed at a 6 percent rate.

Qualified production activities income is generally calculated as a taxpayer's domestic production gross receipts (i.e., the gross receipts derived from any lease, rental, license, sale, exchange, or other disposition of qualifying production property manufactured, produced, grown, or extracted by the taxpayer in whole or significant part within the United States; any qualified film produced by the taxpayer; or electricity, natural gas, or potable water produced by the taxpayer in the United States) minus the cost of goods sold and other expenses, losses, or deductions attributable to such receipts.

The manufacturing deduction generally is available to all taxpayers that generate qualified production activities income, which under current law includes income from the sale, exchange or disposition of oil, natural gas or primary products thereof produced in the United States.

Reasons for Change

The President agreed at the G-20 Summit in Pittsburgh to phase out subsidies for fossil fuels so that the United States can transition to a 21st century energy economy. The manufacturing deduction effectively provides a lower rate of tax with respect to a favored source of income. The lower rate of tax, like other oil and gas preferences the Administration proposes to repeal, distorts markets by encouraging more investment in the oil and gas industry than would occur under a neutral system. To the extent the lower tax rate encourages overproduction of oil and gas, it is detrimental to long-term energy security and is also inconsistent with the Administration's policy of reducing carbon emissions and encouraging the use of renewable energy sources. Moreover, the tax subsidy for oil and gas must ultimately be financed with taxes that result in underinvestment in other, potentially more productive, areas of the economy.

Proposal

The proposal would exclude from the definition of domestic production gross receipts all gross receipts derived from the sale, exchange or other disposition of oil, natural gas or a primary product thereof for taxable years beginning after December 31, 2010.

INCREASE GEOLOGICAL AND GEOPHYSICAL AMORTIZATION PERIOD FOR INDEPENDENT PRODUCERS TO SEVEN YEARS

Current Law

Geological and geophysical expenditures are costs incurred for the purpose of obtaining and accumulating data that will serve as the basis for the acquisition and retention of mineral properties. The amortization period for geological and geophysical expenditures incurred in connection with oil and gas exploration in the United States is two years for independent producers and seven years for integrated oil and gas producers.

Reasons for Change

The President agreed at the G-20 Summit in Pittsburgh to phase out subsidies for fossil fuels so that the United States can transition to a 21st century energy economy. The accelerated amortization of geological and geophysical expenditures incurred by independent producers, like other oil and gas preferences the Administration proposes to repeal, distorts markets by encouraging more investment in the oil and gas industry than would occur under a neutral system. To the extent accelerated amortization encourages overproduction of oil and gas, it is detrimental to long-term energy security and is also inconsistent with the Administration's policy of reducing carbon emissions and encouraging the use of renewable energy sources. Moreover, the tax subsidy for oil and gas must ultimately be financed with taxes that result in underinvestment in other, potentially more productive, areas of the economy.

Increasing the amortization period for geological and geophysical expenditures incurred by independent oil and gas producers from two years to seven years would provide a more accurate reflection of their income and more consistent tax treatment for all oil and gas producers.

Proposal

The proposal would increase the amortization period from two years to seven years for geological and geophysical expenditures incurred by independent producers in connection with all oil and gas exploration in the United States. Seven-year amortization would apply even if the property is abandoned and any remaining basis of the abandoned property would be recovered over the remainder of the seven-year period. The proposal would be effective for amounts paid or incurred after December 31, 2010.

Eliminate Coal Preferences

REPEAL EXPENSING OF EXPLORATION AND DEVELOPMENT COSTS

Current Law

In general, costs that benefit future periods must be capitalized and recovered over such periods for income tax purposes, rather than being expensed in the period the costs are incurred. In addition, the uniform capitalization rules require certain direct and indirect costs allocable to property to be included in inventory or capitalized as part of the basis of such property. In general, the uniform capitalization rules apply to real and tangible personal property produced by the taxpayer or acquired for resale.

Special rules apply in the case of mining exploration and development expenditures. A taxpayer may elect to expense the exploration costs incurred for the purpose of ascertaining the existence, location, extent, or quality of an ore or mineral deposit, including a deposit of coal or other hard mineral fossil fuel. Exploration costs that are expensed are recaptured when the mine reaches the producing stage either by a reduction in depletion deductions or, at the election of the taxpayer, by an inclusion in income in the year in which the mine reaches the producing stage.

After the existence of a commercially marketable deposit has been disclosed, costs incurred for the development of a mine to exploit the deposit are deductible in the year paid or incurred unless the taxpayer elects to deduct the costs on a ratable basis as the minerals or ores produced from the deposit are sold.

In the case of a corporation that elects to deduct exploration costs in the year paid or incurred, 30 percent of the otherwise deductible costs must be capitalized and amortized over a 60-month period. In addition, a taxpayer that has elected to deduct exploration costs may, nevertheless, elect to capitalize and amortize certain intangible drilling costs over a 60-month period beginning with the month the expenditure was paid or incurred. This rule applies on an expenditure-by-expenditure basis; that is, for any particular taxable year, a taxpayer may deduct some portion of its exploration costs and capitalize the rest under this provision. This allows the taxpayer to reduce or eliminate adjustments or preferences for exploration costs under the alternative minimum tax. Similar rules limiting corporate deductions and providing for 60-month amortization apply with respect to mine development costs.

The election to deduct exploration costs and the rule making development costs deductible in the year paid or incurred apply only with respect to domestic ore and mineral deposits.

Reasons for Change

The President agreed at the G-20 Summit in Pittsburgh to phase out subsidies for fossil fuels so that the United States can transition to a 21st century energy economy. The expensing of exploration and development costs relating to coal and other hard mineral fossil fuels, like other fossil fuel preferences the Administration proposes to repeal, distorts markets by encouraging more investment in fossil fuel production than would occur under a neutral system. To the extent expensing encourages overproduction of coal and other hard mineral fossil fuels, it is inconsistent with the Administration's policy of reducing carbon emissions and encouraging the use of renewable energy sources. Moreover, the tax subsidy for coal and other hard mineral fossil fuels must ultimately be financed with taxes that result in underinvestment in other, potentially more productive, areas of the economy. Capitalization of exploration and development costs relating to coal and other hard mineral fossil fuels would place taxpayers in that industry on a cost recovery system similar to that employed by other industries and reduce economic distortions.

Proposal

Expensing and 60-month amortization of exploration and development costs relating to coal and other hard mineral fossil fuels would not be allowed. The costs would be capitalized as depreciable or depletable property, depending on the nature of the cost incurred, in accordance with the generally applicable rules. The other hard mineral fossil fuels for which expensing and 60-month amortization would not be allowed include lignite and oil shale to which a 15-percent depletion rate applies.

The proposal would be effective for costs paid or incurred after December 31, 2010.

REPEAL PERCENTAGE DEPLETION FOR HARD MINERAL FOSSIL FUELS

Current Law

The capital costs of coal mines and other hard mineral fossil fuel properties are recovered through the depletion deduction. Under the cost depletion method, the basis recovery for a taxable year is proportional to the exhaustion of the property during the year. This method does not permit cost recovery deductions that exceed basis or that are allowable on an accelerated basis.

A taxpayer may also qualify for percentage depletion with respect to coal and other hard mineral fossil fuel properties. The amount of the deduction is a statutory percentage of the gross income from the property. The percentage is 10 percent for coal and lignite and 15 percent for oil shale (other than oil shale to which a 7 ½ percent depletion rate applies because it is used for certain nonfuel purposes). The deduction may not exceed 50 percent of the taxable income from the property (determined before the deductions for depletion and domestic manufacturing).

A qualifying taxpayer determines the depletion deduction for each oil and gas property under both the percentage depletion method and the cost depletion method and deducts the larger of the two amounts. Because percentage depletion is computed without regard to the taxpayer's basis in the depletable property, a taxpayer may continue to claim percentage depletion after all the expenditures incurred to acquire and develop the property have been recovered.

Reasons for Change

The President agreed at the G-20 Summit in Pittsburgh to phase out subsidies for fossil fuels so that the United States can transition to a 21st century energy economy. Percentage depletion effectively provides a lower rate of tax with respect to a favored source of income. The lower rate of tax, like other fossil fuel preferences the Administration proposes to repeal, distorts markets by encouraging more investment in fossil fuel production than would occur under a neutral system. To the extent the lower tax rate encourages overproduction of coal and other hard mineral fossil fuels, it is inconsistent with the Administration's policy of reducing carbon emissions and encouraging the use of renewable energy sources. Moreover, the tax subsidy for coal and other hard mineral fossil fuels must ultimately be financed with taxes that result in underinvestment in other, potentially more productive, areas of the economy.

Cost depletion computed by reference to the taxpayer's basis in the property is the equivalent of economic depreciation. Limiting fossil fuel producers to cost depletion would place them on a cost recovery system similar to that employed by other industries and reduce economic distortions.

Proposal

Percentage depletion would not be allowed with respect to coal and other hard mineral fossil fuels. The other hard mineral fossil fuels for which no percentage depletion would be allowed include lignite and oil shale to which a 15-percent depletion rate applies. Taxpayers would be permitted to claim cost depletion on their adjusted basis, if any, in coal and other hard mineral fossil fuel properties.

The proposal would be effective for taxable years beginning after December 31, 2010.

REPEAL CAPITAL GAINS TREATMENT OF CERTAIN ROYALTIES

Current Law

Royalties received on the disposition of coal or lignite generally qualify for treatment as long-term capital gain, and the royalty owner does not qualify for percentage depletion with respect to the coal or lignite. This treatment does not apply unless the taxpayer has been the owner of the mineral in place for at least one year before it is mined. The treatment also does not apply to income realized as a co-adventurer, partner, or principal in the mining of the mineral or to certain related party transactions.

Reasons for Change

The President agreed at the G-20 Summit in Pittsburgh to phase out subsidies for fossil fuels so that the United States can transition to a 21st century energy economy. The capital gain treatment of coal and lignite royalties, like other fossil fuel preferences the Administration proposes to repeal, distorts markets by encouraging more investment in fossil fuel production than would occur under a neutral system. To the extent capital gains treatment encourages overproduction of coal and lignite, it is inconsistent with the Administration's policy of reducing carbon emissions and encouraging the use of renewable energy sources. Moreover, the tax subsidy for coal and lignite must ultimately be financed with taxes that result in underinvestment in other, potentially more productive, areas of the economy.

Proposal

The capital gain treatment of coal and lignite royalties would be repealed and the royalties would be taxed as ordinary income.

The proposal would be effective for amounts realized in taxable years beginning after December 31, 2010.

REPEAL DOMESTIC MANUFACTURING DEDUCTION FOR COAL AND OTHER HARD MINERAL FOSSIL FUELS

Current Law

A deduction is allowed with respect to income attributable to domestic production activities (the manufacturing deduction). For taxable years beginning after 2009, the manufacturing deduction is generally equal to 9 percent of the lesser of qualified production activities income for the taxable year or taxable income for the taxable year, limited to 50 percent of the W-2 wages of the taxpayer for the taxable year.

Qualified production activities income is generally calculated as a taxpayer's domestic production gross receipts (i.e., the gross receipts derived from any lease, rental, license, sale, exchange, or other disposition of qualifying production property manufactured, produced, grown, or extracted by the taxpayer in whole or significant part within the United States; any qualified film produced by the taxpayer; or electricity, natural gas, or potable water produced by the taxpayer in the United States) minus the cost of goods sold and other expenses, losses, or deductions attributable to such receipts.

The manufacturing deduction generally is available to all taxpayers that generate qualified production activities income, which under current law includes income from the sale, exchange or disposition of coal, other hard mineral fossil fuels, or primary products thereof produced in the United States.

Reasons for Change

The President agreed at the G-20 Summit in Pittsburgh to phase out subsidies for fossil fuels so that the United States can transition to a 21st century energy economy. The manufacturing deduction effectively provides a lower rate of tax with respect to a favored source of income. The lower rate of tax, like other fossil fuel preferences the Administration proposes to repeal, distorts markets by encouraging more investment in fossil fuel production than would occur under a neutral system. To the extent the lower tax rate encourages overproduction of coal and other hard mineral fossil fuels, it is inconsistent with the Administration's policy of reducing carbon emissions and encouraging the use of renewable energy sources. Moreover, the tax subsidy for coal and other hard mineral fossil fuels must ultimately be financed with taxes that result in underinvestment in other, potentially more productive, areas of the economy.

Proposal

The proposal would exclude from the definition of domestic production gross receipts all gross receipts derived from the sale, exchange or other disposition of coal, other hard mineral fossil fuels, or a primary product thereof. The hard mineral fossil fuels to which the exclusion would apply include lignite and oil shale to which a 15-percent depletion rate applies.

The proposal would be effective for taxable years beginning after December 31, 2010.

ADDITIONAL REVENUE CHANGES

TAX CARRIED (PROFITS) INTERESTS AS ORDINARY INCOME

Current Law

A partnership is not subject to Federal income tax. Instead, an item of income or loss of the partnership retains its character and flows through to the partners, who must include such item on their tax returns. Generally, certain partners receive partnership interests in exchange for contributions of cash and/or property, while certain partners (not necessarily other partners) receive partnership interests, typically interests in future profits ("profits interests" or "carried interests"), in exchange for services. Accordingly, if and to the extent a partnership recognizes long-term capital gain, the partners, including partners who provide services, will reflect their shares of such gain on their tax returns as long-term capital gain. If the partner is an individual, such gain would be taxed at the reduced rates for long-term capital gains. Gain recognized on the sale of a partnership interest, whether it was received in exchange for property, cash or services, is generally treated as capital gain.

Under current law, income attributable to a profits interest of a general partner is generally subject to self-employment tax, except to the extent the partnership generates types of income that are excluded from self-employment taxes, e.g., capital gains, certain interest, and dividends.

Reason for Change

Although profits interests are structured as partnership interests, the income allocable to such interests is received in connection with the performance of services. A service provider's share of the income of a partnership attributable to a carried interest should be taxed as ordinary income and subject to self-employment tax because such income is derived from the performance of services. By allowing service partners to receive capital gains treatment on labor income without limit, the current system creates an unfair and inefficient tax preference. The recent explosion of activity among large private equity firms and hedge funds has increased the breadth and cost of this tax preference, with some of the highest-income Americans benefiting from the preferential treatment.

Proposal

A partner's share of income on a "services partnership interest" (SPI) would be subject to tax as ordinary income, regardless of the character of the income at the partnership level. Accordingly, such income would not be eligible for the reduced rates that apply to long-term capital gains. In addition, the proposal would require the partner to pay self-employment taxes on such income. Gain recognized on the sale of an SPI would generally be taxed as ordinary income, not as capital gain.

An SPI is a carried interest held by a person who provides services to the partnership. To the extent that the partner who holds an SPI contributes "invested capital" and the partnership reasonably allocates its income and loss between such invested capital and the remaining

91

interest, income attributable to the invested capital would not be recharacterized. Similarly, the portion of any gain recognized on the sale of an SPI that is attributable to the invested capital would be treated as capital gain. "Invested capital" is defined as money or other property contributed to the partnership. However, contributed capital that is attributable to the proceeds of any loan or other advance made or guaranteed by any partner or the partnership is not treated as "invested capital."

Also, any person who performs services for an entity and holds a "disqualified interest" in the entity is subject to tax at rates applicable to ordinary income on any income or gain received with respect to the interest. A "disqualified interest" is defined as convertible or contingent debt, an option, or any derivative instrument with respect to the entity (but does not include a partnership interest or stock in certain taxable corporations). This is an anti-abuse rule designed to prevent the avoidance of the proposal through the use of compensatory arrangements other than partnership interests. Other anti-abuse rules may be necessary.

The proposal is not intended to adversely affect qualification of a real estate investment trust owning a carried interest in a real estate partnership.

The proposal would be effective for taxable years beginning after December 31, 2010.

MODIFY THE CELLULOSIC BIOFUEL PRODUCER CREDIT

An income tax credit is allowed for cellulosic biofuel that is produced by the taxpayer. The cellulosic biofuel producer credit is $1.01 per gallon reduced, in the case of an alcohol cellulosic biofuel, by the alcohol credit allowable with respect to the fuel.

Cellulosic biofuel is defined as any liquid fuel that (i) is produced from any lignocellulosic or hemicellulosic matter that is available on a renewable or recurring basis and (ii) meets the registration requirements for fuels and fuel additives established by the Environmental Protection Agency under section 211 of the Clean Air Act (EPA registration requirements).

The cellulosic biofuel either (i) must be sold by its producer for use by the purchaser in the production of a qualified cellulosic biofuel mixture in the purchaser's trade or business, for use by the purchaser in the purchaser's trade or business, or for retail sale (and delivery into the retail purchaser's fuel tank) by the purchaser or (ii) must be used or sold by the producer for any such purpose. A qualified cellulosic biofuel mixture is a mixture of cellulosic biofuel with either gasoline or any other fuel suitable for use in an internal combustion engine, but only if the mixture is sold by the person producing the mixture for use as a fuel or is used as a fuel by the person producing the mixture.

The credit is allowed only against the producer's income tax liability. The credit expires on December 31, 2012.

Reasons for Change

Liquid byproducts derived from the processing of paper or pulp (known as black liquor when derived from the kraft process) are produced from lignocellulosic or hemicellulosic matter available on a renewable or recurring basis. Thus, any such liquid byproducts that meet the EPA registration requirements would qualify as cellulosic biofuel and, to the extent so qualifying, would result in substantial revenue losses and a windfall to the paper industry.

Proposal

The Administration proposes to exclude from the definition of cellulosic biofuel any fuels that (i) are more than four percent (by weight) water or sediment in any combination, or (ii) have an ash content of more than one percent (by weight). This change would exclude black liquor from eligibility for the credit.

The proposal would be effective on the date of enactment.

ELIMINATE THE ADVANCED EARNED INCOME TAX CREDIT

Current Law

Under current law, low- and moderate-income individuals may be eligible for the refundable earned income tax credit (EITC). The amount of EITC an eligible individual may claim is a function of income and earnings, the number of children in the household, and filing status. In 2010, families with one child are eligible for a maximum EITC of $3,050. Eligible individuals with more children receive a larger credit.

Since 1978, most eligible individuals have had the option of requesting advance payments of the EITC from their employers throughout the year. Self-employed and childless individuals are not eligible. Under current law, the advance payment is limited to 60 percent of the maximum credit to which a worker with one child would be entitled. In 2010, the maximum advance payment is $1,830.

Employers offset the costs of the advance payments by reducing their payments of withheld income and employment taxes. During the year, employers periodically notify the IRS of the aggregate amount of advance payments withheld from tax payments. After the year is over, the employer notifies the Internal Revenue Service of employees' receipts of advance payments. The information is also provided to the employees. Upon filing their tax returns, individuals must reconcile any advance payments received during the year with the amount of EITC for which they actually were eligible. If they received too little, they can obtain the remaining amount; conversely, if they received too much, they must repay the overpayment with their tax return. Individuals who have received an advance payment are required to file a tax return, even if their income is below the filing threshold. In view of the risk of overpayments, the advance payment is limited to 60 percent of the one-child maximum credit.

Reason for Change

The advance payment option provides a mechanism for individuals to receive payments on a timely basis, instead of as a single payment during the filing season. Advance payments could help cash-constrained households meet their daily needs. However, advance payments have been extremely unpopular among eligible taxpayers – at most, 3 percent of eligible individuals participate, and IRS' efforts to increase participation have not had a meaningful impact. Furthermore, recent research shows evidence of significant non-compliance by employers and workers. As a consequence, repealing the advance payment option would adversely affect few individuals who are eligible for this benefit.

Proposal

The proposal would repeal the advance payment option of the EITC. Workers would no longer be able to receive an advance payment of their expected EITC through their employer. (Individuals with positive tax liability would still be able to receive any non-refundable portion of the EITC during the year through adjustments in their withholding.)

The proposal would be effective for taxable years beginning after December 31, 2010.

DENY DEDUCTION FOR PUNITIVE DAMAGES

Current Law

No deduction is allowed for a fine or similar penalty paid to a government for the violation of any law. If a taxpayer is convicted of a violation of the antitrust laws, or the taxpayer's plea of guilty or nolo contendere to such a violation is entered or accepted in a criminal proceeding, no deduction is allowed for two-thirds of any amount paid or incurred on a judgment or in settlement of a civil suit brought under section 4 of the Clayton Antitrust Act on account of such or any related antitrust violation. Where neither of these two provisions is applicable, a deduction is allowed for damages paid or incurred as ordinary and necessary expenses in carrying on any trade or business, regardless of whether such damages are compensatory or punitive.

Reasons for Change

The deductibility of punitive damage payments undermines the role of such damages in discouraging and penalizing certain undesirable actions or activities.

Proposal

No deduction would be allowed for punitive damages paid or incurred by the taxpayer, whether upon a judgment or in settlement of a claim. Where the liability for punitive damages is covered by insurance, such damages paid or incurred by the insurer would be included in the gross income of the insured person. The insurer would be required to report such payments to the insured person and to the Internal Revenue Service.

The proposal would apply to damages paid or incurred after December 31, 2011.

REPEAL LOWER-OF-COST-OR-MARKET INVENTORY ACCOUNTING METHOD

Current Law

Taxpayers required to maintain inventories are permitted to use a variety of methods to determine the cost of their ending inventories, including methods such as the last-in, first-out ("LIFO") method, the first-in, first-out ("FIFO") method, and the retail method. Taxpayers not using a LIFO method may write down the carrying values of their inventories by applying the lower-of-cost-or-market ("LCM") method and may write down the cost of "subnormal" goods (i.e., those that are unsalable at normal prices or unusable in the normal way because of damage, imperfection or other similar causes).

Reasons for Change

The allowance of inventory write-downs under the LCM and subnormal goods provisions is an exception from the realization principle, and is essentially a one-way mark-to-market regime that understates taxable income. Thus, a taxpayer is able to obtain a larger cost-of-goods-sold deduction by writing down an item of inventory if its replacement cost falls, but need not increase an item's inventory value if its replacement cost increases. This asymmetric treatment is unwarranted. Also, the market value used under LCM for tax purposes generally is the replacement or reproduction cost of an item of inventory, not the item's net realizable value, as is required under generally accepted financial accounting rules. While the operation of the retail method is technically symmetric, it also allows retailers to obtain deductions for write-downs below inventory cost because of normal and anticipated declines in retail prices.

Proposal

The proposal would statutorily prohibit the use of the LCM and subnormal goods methods. Appropriate wash-sale rules also would be included to prevent taxpayers from circumventing the prohibition. The proposal would result in a change in the method of accounting for inventories for taxpayers currently using the LCM and subnormal goods methods, and any resulting section 481(a) adjustment generally would be included in income ratably over a four-year period beginning with the year of change.

The proposal would be effective for taxable years beginning after twelve months from the date of enactment.

REDUCE THE TAX GAP AND MAKE REFORMS

Expand Information Reporting

REQUIRE INFORMATION REPORTING ON PAYMENTS TO CORPORATIONS

Current Law

Generally, a taxpayer making payments to a recipient aggregating to $600 or more for services or determinable gains in the course of a trade or business in a calendar year is required to send an information return to the IRS setting forth the amount, as well as name and address of the recipient of the payment (generally on Form 1099). Under a longstanding regulatory regime, there are certain exceptions for payments to corporations, as well as tax-exempt and government entities.

Reasons for Change

Generally, compliance increases significantly for payments that a third party reports to the IRS. In the case of tax-exempt or government entities that are generally not subject to income tax, information returns may not be necessary. On the other hand, during the decades in which the regulatory exception for payments to corporations has become established, the number and complexity of corporate taxpayers have increased. Moreover, the longstanding regulatory exception from information reporting for payments to corporations has created compliance issues. Although the exception for information reporting to corporations is set forth in existing regulations, because it has been in place for many years and because Congress, during that time period, has made numerous changes to the information reporting rules, elimination of the exception should be made by legislative change.

Proposal

A business would generally be required to file an information return for payments for services or for determinable gains aggregating to $600 or more in a calendar year to a corporation (except a tax-exempt corporation). Regulatory authority would be provided to make appropriate exceptions where reporting would be especially burdensome.

The proposal would be effective for payments made to corporations after December 31, 2010.

REQUIRE INFORMATION REPORTING FOR RENTAL PROPERTY EXPENSE PAYMENTS

Current Law

Generally, a taxpayer making payments in the course of a trade or business to a noncorporate recipient aggregating to $600 or more for services or determinable gains in a calendar year is required to send an information return to the IRS setting forth the amount, as well as name and address of the recipient of the payment (generally on Form 1099). If the taxpayer making payments is not engaged in a trade or business, such information reporting is not required.

At present, there is limited third-party information reporting related to rental real estate expenses because only taxpayers whose rental real estate activity is considered a trade or business are required to report payments. Additionally, whether a taxpayer's rental real estate activity should be considered a trade or business requires a case-by-case analysis that depends on the facts and circumstances of each taxpayer.

Reasons for Change

Information reporting requirements generally improve taxpayer compliance. Requiring information reporting by taxpayers receiving rental income and deducting expenses on rental activities would improve the reporting compliance by taxpayers providing services to those rental activities. In addition, increased third-party reporting of major rental expenses is likely to improve reporting compliance on rental real estate income.

Proposal

The proposal would, in general, subject recipients of rental income from real estate to the same information reporting requirements as those applicable to taxpayers engaging in a trade or business. In particular, rental income recipients making payments of $600 or more to a service provider (such as a plumber, painter, or accountant) in the course of earning rental income would be required to send an information return, generally a Form 1099-MISC, to the IRS and to the service provider. Exceptions to the reporting requirement would be made for particularly burdensome situations, such as for taxpayers (including members of the military) who rent their principal residence on a temporary basis, or for those who receive only small amounts of rental income.

The proposal would be effective for taxable years beginning after December 31, 2010.

REQUIRE INFORMATION REPORTING FOR PRIVATE SEPARATE ACCOUNTS OF LIFE INSURANCE COMPANIES

Current Law

Earnings from direct investment in securities generally result in taxable income to the holder. In contrast, investments in comparable assets through a separate account of a life insurance company generally give rise to tax-free or tax-deferred income. This favorable tax treatment for investing through a life insurance company is not available if the policyholder has so much control over the investments in the separate account that the policyholder, rather than the insurance company, is treated as the owner of those investments.

Reasons for Change

In some cases, private separate accounts are being used to avoid tax that would be due if the assets were held directly. Better reporting of investments in private separate accounts will help the IRS to ensure that income is properly reported. Moreover, such reporting will enable the IRS to identify more easily which variable insurance contracts qualify as insurance contracts under current law and which contracts should be disregarded under the investor control doctrine.

Proposal

The proposal would require life insurance companies to report to the IRS, for each contract whose cash value is partially or wholly invested in a private separate account for any portion of the taxable year and represents at least 10 percent of the value of the account, the policyholder's taxpayer identification number, the policy number, the amount of accumulated untaxed income, the total contract account value, and the portion of that value that was invested in one or more private separate accounts. For this purpose, a private separate account would be defined as any account with respect to which a related group of persons owns policies whose cash values, in the aggregate, represent at least 10 percent of the value of the separate account. Whether a related group of persons owns policies whose cash values represent at least 10 percent of the value of the account would be determined quarterly, based on information reasonably within the issuer's possession.

The proposal would be effective for taxable years beginning after December 31, 2010.

REQUIRE A CERTIFIED TAXPAYER IDENTIFICATION NUMBER FROM CONTRACTORS AND ALLOW CERTAIN WITHHOLDING

Current Law

In the course of a trade or business, service recipients ("businesses") making payments aggregating to $600 or more in a calendar year to any non-employee service provider ("contractor") that is not a corporation are required to send an information return to the IRS setting forth the amount, as well as name, address, and taxpayer identification number (TIN) of the contractor. The information returns, required annually after the end of the year, are made on Form 1099-MISC based on identifying information furnished by the contractor but not verified by the IRS. Copies are provided both to the contractor and to the IRS. Withholding is not required or permitted for payments to contractors. Since contractors are not subject to withholding, they may be required to make quarterly payments of estimated income taxes and self-employment (SECA) taxes near the end of each calendar quarter. The contractor is required to pay any balance due when the annual income tax return is subsequently filed.

Reasons for Change

Without accurate taxpayer identifying information, information reporting requirements impose avoidable burdens on businesses and the IRS, and cannot reach their potential to improve compliance.

Estimated tax filing is relatively burdensome, especially for less sophisticated and lower-income taxpayers. Moreover, by the time estimated tax payments (or final tax payments) are due, some contractors will not have put aside the necessary funds. Given that the SECA tax rate is 15.3 percent (up to certain income limits), the required estimated tax payments can be more than 25 percent of a contractor's gross receipts, even for a contractor with modest income.

An optional withholding method for contractors would reduce the burdens of having to make quarterly payments, would help contractors automatically set aside funds for tax payments, and would help increase compliance.

Proposal

A contractor receiving payments of $600 or more in a calendar year from a particular business would be required to furnish to the business (on Form W-9) the contractor's certified TIN. A business would be required to verify the contractor's TIN with the IRS, which would be authorized to disclose, solely for this purpose, whether the certified TIN-name combination matches IRS records. If a contractor failed to furnish an accurate certified TIN, the business would be required to withhold a flat-rate percentage of gross payments. Contractors receiving payments of $600 or more in a calendar year from a particular business could require the business to withhold a flat-rate percentage of their gross payments, with the flat-rate percentage of 15, 25, 30, or 35 percent being selected by the contractor.

The proposal would be effective for payments made to contractors after December 31, 2010.

REQUIRE INCREASED INFORMATION REPORTING FOR CERTAIN GOVERNMENT PAYMENTS FOR PROPERTY AND SERVICES

Current Law

Businesses, governments, and other taxpayers are subject to a number of information reporting and withholding requirements. Generally, a taxpayer making payments aggregating to $600 or more for services or determinable gains in the course of a trade or business in a calendar year is required to send an information return to the IRS (except if the recipient is a corporation) setting forth the amount, as well as the name and address of the recipient of the payment (generally on Form 1099). In addition, any service recipient engaged in a trade or business is required to file an information return if the aggregate of payments for services is $600 or more in a calendar year. This requirement specifically applies to government agencies, even if the service provider is a corporation. Moreover, Federal agencies must file information returns with respect to contractors, generally on Form 8596 (Information Return for Federal Contracts) and Form 8596A (Quarterly Transmittal of Information Returns for Federal Contracts). Under recently enacted legislation that will take effect in 2012, Federal, State and local government agencies generally must withhold 3 percent of payments for goods or services. Exceptions apply to certain payments such as those actually subjected to backup withholding, wages and public assistance.

Reasons for Change

Generally, compliance increases significantly for payments that a third party reports to the IRS. Some government vendors fail to meet their tax filing and payment obligations.

Proposal

The IRS and Treasury Department would be authorized to promulgate regulations requiring information reporting on all non-wage payments by Federal, State and local governments to procure property or services. It is expected that certain categories of payments would be excluded from the new information reporting requirements, including payments of interest, payments for real property, payments to tax-exempt entities or foreign governments, intergovernmental payments, and payments made pursuant to a classified or confidential contract.

The proposal would be effective for payments made after December 31, 2010.

INCREASE INFORMATION RETURN PENALTIES

Current Law

There are a number of information reporting requirements under the Code. When these requirements are not followed, penalties may apply based on whether and when a correct information return is filed. If a person subject to the information reporting requirements files a correct information return after the prescribed filing date, but on or before the date that is thirty days after the prescribed filing date, the amount of the penalty is $15 per return (the "first-tier penalty"), not to exceed $75,000 per calendar year. If such a person files a correct information return more than thirty days after the prescribed filing date but on or before August 1, the amount of the penalty is $30 per return (the "second-tier penalty"), not to exceed $150,000 per calendar year. If such a person does not file a correct information return on or before August 1, the amount of the penalty is $50 per return (the "third-tier penalty"), not to exceed $250,000 in a calendar year. For certain small filers whose average annual gross receipts do not exceed $5,000,000, the maximum calendar year limit is $25,000 (instead of $75,000) for the first-tier penalty, $50,000 (instead of $150,000) for the second-tier penalty, and $100,000 (instead of $250,000) for the third-tier penalty. If a failure is due to intentional disregard of a filing requirement, the minimum penalty for each failure is $100, with no calendar year limit.

Reasons for Change

Generally, compliance increases significantly with respect to amounts reported on information returns. In some cases, filers may have failed to comply with existing information reporting requirements because the amount of the potentially applicable penalties is too small to discourage non-compliance. Increasing the penalty amounts, which were established in 1989 and have not been increased, will help to ensure the timely filing of accurate information returns.

Proposal

The first-tier penalty would be increased from $15 to $30, and the calendar year maximum would be increased from $75,000 to $250,000. The second-tier penalty would be increased from $30 to $60, and the calendar year maximum would be increased from $150,000 to $500,000. The third-tier penalty would be increased from $50 to $100, and the calendar year maximum would be increased from $250,000 to $1,500,000. For small filers, the calendar year maximum would be increased from $25,000 to $75,000 for the first-tier penalty, from $50,000 to $200,000 for the second-tier penalty, and from $100,000 to $500,000 for the third-tier penalty. The minimum penalty for each failure due to intentional disregard would be increased from $100 to $250. The proposal would also provide that every five years the penalty amounts would be adjusted to account for inflation.

The proposal would be effective for information returns required to be filed after December 31, 2011.

Improve Compliance by Business

REQUIRE GREATER ELECTRONIC FILING OF RETURNS

Current Law

Corporations with assets of $10 million or more filing Form 1120 are required to file Schedule M-3 (Net Income (Loss) Reconciliation for Corporations with Total Assets of $10 Million or More). This Schedule M-3 filing requirement also applies to S corporations, life insurance corporations, property and casualty insurance corporations, and cooperative associations filing various versions of Form 1120 and having $10 million or more in assets. Schedule M-3 is also required for partnerships with assets of $10 million or more and certain other partnerships.

Corporations and tax-exempt organizations that have assets of $10 million or more and file at least 250 returns during a calendar year, including income tax, information, excise tax, and employment tax returns, are required to file electronically their Form 1120/1120S income tax returns and Form 990 information returns. In addition, private foundations and charitable trusts that file at least 250 returns during a calendar year are required to file electronically their Form 990-PF information returns, regardless of their asset size. Taxpayers can request waivers of the electronic filing requirement if they cannot meet that requirement due to technological constraints, or if compliance with the requirement would result in undue financial burden on the taxpayer. Although electronic filing is required of certain corporations and other taxpayers, others may convert voluntarily to electronic filing.

Generally, regulations may require electronic filing by taxpayers (other than individuals, estates and trusts) that file at least 250 returns annually. Before requiring electronic filing, the IRS and Treasury Department must take into account the ability of taxpayers to comply at a reasonable cost.

Reasons for Change

Generally, compliance increases when taxpayers are required to provide better information to the IRS in usable form. Large organizations with assets of $10 million or more generally maintain financial records in electronic form, and generally either hire tax professionals who use tax preparation software or use tax preparation software themselves although they may not currently file electronically.

Electronic filing supports the broader goals of improving IRS service to taxpayers, enhancing compliance, and modernizing tax administration. Overall, increased electronic filing of returns may improve customer satisfaction and confidence in the filing process, and it may be more cost effective for affected entities. Expanding electronic filing to certain additional large entities will help provide tax return information in a more uniform electronic form. This will enhance the ability of the IRS to more productively focus its audit activities. This can reduce burdens on businesses where the need for an audit can be avoided.

In the case of a large business, adopting the same standard for electronic filing as for filing Schedule M-3 provides simplification benefits.

Proposal

All corporations and partnerships required to file Schedule M-3 would be required to file their tax returns electronically. In the case of certain other large taxpayers not required to file Schedule M-3 (such as exempt organizations), the regulatory authority to require electronic filing would be expanded to allow reduction of the current threshold of filing 250 or more returns during a calendar year. Additionally, the regulatory authority would be expanded to allow reduction of the 250-return threshold in the case of information returns such as those required by Subpart B, Part III, Subchapter A, Chapter 61, Subtitle F, of the Internal Revenue Code (generally Forms 1099, 1098, 1096, and 5498). Nevertheless, any new regulations would balance the benefits of electronic filing against any burden that might be imposed on taxpayers, and implementation would take place incrementally to afford adequate time for transition to electronic filing. Taxpayers would be able to request waivers of this requirement if they cannot meet the requirement due to technological constraints, if compliance with the requirement would result in undue financial burden, or if other criteria specified in regulations are met.

The proposal would be effective for taxable years ending after December 31, 2010.

IMPLEMENT STANDARDS CLARIFYING WHEN EMPLOYEE LEASING COMPANIES CAN BE HELD LIABLE FOR THEIR CLIENTS' FEDERAL EMPLOYMENT TAXES

Current Law

Employers are required to withhold and pay Federal Insurance Contribution Act (FICA) taxes and to withhold and remit income taxes, and are required to pay Federal Unemployment Tax Act (FUTA) taxes (collectively "Federal employment taxes") with respect to wages paid to their employees. Liability for Federal employment taxes generally lies with the taxpayer that is determined to be the employer under a multi-factor common law test or under specific statutory provisions. For example, a third party that is not the common law employer can be a statutory employer if the third party has control over the payment of wages. In addition, certain designated agents are jointly and severally liable with their principals for employment taxes with respect to wages paid to the principals' employees. These designated agents prepare and file employment tax returns using their own name and employer identification number. In contrast, reporting agents (often referred to as payroll service providers) are generally not liable for the employment taxes reported on their clients' returns. Reporting agents prepare and file employment tax returns for their clients using the client's name and employer identification number.

Employee leasing is the practice of contracting with an outside business to handle certain administrative, personnel, and payroll matters for a taxpayer's employees. Employee leasing companies (often referred to as professional employer organizations) typically prepare and file employment tax returns for their clients using the leasing company's name and employer identification number, often taking the position that the leasing company is the statutory or common law employer of their clients' workers.

Reasons for Change

Under present law, there is often uncertainty as to whether the employee leasing company or its client is liable for unpaid Federal employment taxes arising with respect to wages paid to the client's workers. Thus, when an employee leasing company files employment tax returns using its own name and employer identification number, but fails to pay some or all of the taxes due, or when no returns are filed with respect to wages paid by a taxpayer that uses an employee leasing company, there can be uncertainty as to how the Federal employment taxes are assessed and collected.

Providing standards for when an employee leasing company and its clients will be held liable for Federal employment taxes will facilitate the assessment, payment and collection of those taxes and will preclude taxpayers who have control over withholding and payment of those taxes from denying liability when the taxes are not paid.

Proposal

The proposal would set forth standards for holding employee leasing companies jointly and severally liable with their clients for Federal employment taxes. The proposal would also provide standards for holding employee leasing companies solely liable for such taxes if they meet specified requirements.

The provision would be effective for employment tax returns required to be filed with respect to wages paid after December 31, 2010.

INCREASE CERTAINTY WITH RESPECT TO WORKER CLASSIFICATION

Current Law

For both tax and nontax purposes, workers must be classified into one of two mutually exclusive categories: employees or self-employed (sometimes referred to as independent contractors).

Worker classification generally is based on a common-law test for determining whether an employment relationship exists. The main determinant is whether the service recipient (employer) has the right to control not only the result of the worker's services but also the means by which the worker accomplishes that result. For classification purposes, it does not matter whether the service recipient exercises that control, only that he or she has the right to exercise it. Even though it is generally recognized that more highly skilled workers may not require much guidance or direction from the service recipient, the underlying concept of the right to control is the same for them. In addition, only individuals can be employees. In determining worker status, the IRS looks to three categories of evidence that may be relevant in determining whether the requisite control exists under the common-law test: behavioral control, financial control, and the relationship of the parties.

For employees, employers are required to withhold income and Federal Insurance Contribution Act (FICA) taxes and to pay the employer's share of FICA taxes. Employers are also required to pay Federal Unemployment Tax Act (FUTA) taxes and generally state unemployment compensation taxes. Liability for Federal employment taxes and the obligation to report the wages generally lie with the employer.

For workers who are classified as independent contractors, service recipients engaged in a trade or business and that make payments totaling $600 or more in a calendar year to an independent contractor that is not a corporation are required to send an information return to the IRS and to the independent contractor stating the total payments made during the year. The service recipient generally does not need to withhold taxes from the payments reported unless the independent contractor has not provided its taxpayer identification number to the service recipient. Independent contractors pay self-employment (SECA) tax on their net earnings from self-employment (which generally is equivalent to both the employer and employee shares of FICA tax). Independent contractors generally are required to pay their income tax, including SECA liabilities, by making quarterly estimated tax payments.

For workers, whether employee or independent contractor status is more beneficial depends on many factors including the extent to which an independent contractor is able to negotiate for gross payments that include the value of nonwage costs that the service provider would have to incur in the case of an employee. In some circumstances, independent contractor status is more beneficial; in other circumstances, employee status is more advantageous.

Under a special provision (section 530 of the Revenue Act of 1978 which was not made part of the Internal Revenue Code), a service recipient may treat a worker as an independent contractor for Federal employment tax purposes even though the worker actually may be an employee under the common law rules if the service recipient has a reasonable basis for treating the worker as an independent contractor and certain other requirements are met. The special provision applies only if (1) the service recipient has not treated the worker (or any worker in a substantially similar position) as an employee for any period beginning after 1977 and (2) the service recipient has filed all Federal tax returns, including all required information returns, on a basis consistent with treating the worker as an independent contractor.

If an employer meets the requirements for the special provision with respect to a class of workers, the IRS is prohibited from reclassifying the workers as employees, even prospectively and even as to newly hired workers in the same class. Since 1996, the IRS has considered the availability of the special provision as the first part of any examination concerning worker classification. If the IRS determines that the special provision applies to a class of workers, it does not determine whether the workers are in fact employees or independent contractors. Thus, the worker classification continues indefinitely even if it incorrect.

The special provision also prohibits the IRS from issuing generally applicable guidance addressing the proper classification of workers. Current law and procedures also provide for reduced penalties for misclassification where the special provision is not available but where, among other things, the employer agrees to prospective reclassification of the workers as employees.

Reasons for Change

Since 1978, the IRS has not been permitted to issue general guidance addressing worker classification, and in many instances has been precluded from reclassifying workers – even prospectively – who may have been misclassified. Since 1978 there have been many changes in working relationships between service providers and service recipients. As a result, there has been continued and growing uncertainty about the correct classification of some workers.

Many benefits and worker protections are available only for workers who are classified as employees. Incorrect classification as an independent contractor for tax purposes may spill over to other areas and, for example, lead to a worker not receiving benefits for unemployment (unemployment insurance) or on-the-job injuries (workers' compensation), or not being protected by various on-the-job health and safety requirements.

The incorrect classification of workers also creates opportunities for competitive advantages over service recipients who properly classify their workers. Such misclassification may lower the service recipient's total cost of labor by avoiding workers' compensation and unemployment compensation premiums, and could also provide increased opportunities for noncompliance by service providers.

Workers, service recipients, and tax administrators would benefit from reducing uncertainty about worker classification, eliminating potential competitive advantages and incentives to misclassify workers associated with worker misclassification by competitors, and reducing opportunities for noncompliance by workers classified as self-employed, while maintaining the benefits and worker protections associated with an administrative and social policy system that is based on employee status.

Proposal

Under the proposal, the IRS would be permitted to require prospective reclassification of workers who are currently misclassified and whose reclassification has been prohibited under current law. The reduced penalties for misclassification provided under current law would be retained, except that lower penalties would apply only if the service recipient voluntarily reclassifies its workers before being contacted by the IRS or another enforcement agency and if the service recipient had filed all required information returns (Forms 1099) reporting the payments to the independent contractors. For service recipients with only a small number of employees and a small number of misclassified workers, even reduced penalties would be waived if the service recipient (1) had consistently filed Forms 1099 reporting all payments to all misclassified workers and (2) agreed to prospective reclassification of misclassified workers. It is anticipated that, after enactment, new enforcement activity would focus mainly on obtaining the proper worker classification prospectively, since in many cases the proper classification of workers may not have been clear. (Statutory employee or nonemployee treatment as specified under current law would be retained.)

The Department of the Treasury and the IRS also would be permitted to issue generally applicable guidance on the proper classification of workers under common law standards. This would enable service recipients to properly classify workers with much less concern about future IRS examinations. Treasury and the IRS would be directed to issue guidance interpreting common law in a neutral manner recognizing that many workers are, in fact, not employees. Further, Treasury and the IRS would develop guidance that would provide safe harbors and/or rebuttable presumptions, both narrowly defined. To make that guidance clearer and more useful for service recipients, it would generally be industry- or job-specific. Priority for the development of guidance would be given to industries and jobs in which application of the common law test has been particularly problematic, where there has been a history of worker misclassification, or where there have been failures to report compensation paid.

Service recipients would be required to give notice to independent contractors, when they first begin performing services for the service recipient, that explains how they will be classified and the consequences thereof, e.g., tax implications, workers' compensation implications, wage and hour implications.

The IRS would be permitted to disclose to the Department of Labor information about service recipients whose workers are reclassified.

To ease compliance burdens for independent contractors, independent contractors receiving payments totaling $600 or more in a calendar year from a service recipient would be permitted to require the service recipient to withhold for Federal tax purposes a flat rate percentage of their gross payments, with the flat rate percentage being selected by the contractor.

The proposal would be effective upon enactment, but prospective reclassification of those covered by the current special provision would not be effective until the first calendar year beginning at least one year after date of enactment. The transition period could be up to two years for independent contractors with existing written contracts establishing their status.

Strengthen Tax Administration

CODIFY "ECONOMIC SUBSTANCE" DOCTRINE

Current Law

Economic Substance Doctrine. The common-law "economic substance" doctrine generally denies tax benefits from a transaction that does not meaningfully change a taxpayer's economic position, other than tax consequences, even if the transaction literally satisfies the requirements of the Internal Revenue Code. Although courts have applied the economic substance doctrine with increasing frequency, they have not applied it uniformly. Some courts require both (i) a meaningful change to the taxpayer's economic position (referred to as "objective" economic substance), and (ii) a substantial non-tax business purpose, while other courts require only one of the two factors to satisfy the economic substance doctrine. Still other courts consider objective economic substance and business purpose to be only two factors in a general investigation into whether a transaction has economic effects other than tax benefits.

Accuracy-Related Penalties. Current law contains an accuracy-related penalty that applies to an underpayment of tax attributable to a substantial understatement of income tax. The penalty equals 20 percent of the tax underpayment. Except in the case of tax shelters, the penalty may be reduced if (i) the taxpayer's treatment is supported by substantial authority or (ii) the relevant facts were adequately disclosed, and there is a reasonable basis for the item's tax treatment. A separate 20-percent penalty applies to an understatement of income tax attributable to a "listed transaction" or a "reportable transaction" with a significant purpose of tax avoidance or evasion. The penalty rate is increased to 30 percent if the taxpayer has not disclosed the transaction as required by law. Either penalty may be set aside or reduced if the taxpayer can demonstrate that there was "reasonable cause" for the taxpayer's position and that the taxpayer acted in good faith.

Denial of Interest Deduction. Current law denies any deduction for interest paid with respect to a reportable transaction understatement where the relevant facts were not adequately disclosed.

Reason for Change

Clarifying the economic substance doctrine and increasing the penalty for transactions that lack economic substance will further deter transactions designed solely to obtain tax benefits.

Proposal

Clarification of Economic Substance Doctrine. The proposal would clarify that a transaction satisfies the economic substance doctrine only if (i) it changes in a meaningful way (apart from federal tax effects) the taxpayer's economic position, and (ii) the taxpayer has a substantial purpose (other than a federal tax purpose) for entering into the transaction. The proposal would also clarify that a transaction will not be treated as having economic substance solely by reason of a profit potential unless the present value of the reasonably expected pre-tax profit is substantial in relation to the present value of the net federal tax benefits arising from the transaction. The proposal would allow the Treasury Department to publish regulations to carry out the purposes of the proposal.

New Understatement Penalty. The proposal would impose a 30-percent penalty on an understatement of tax attributable to a transaction that lacks economic substance, reduced to 20 percent if there were adequate disclosure of the relevant facts in the taxpayer's return. The proposed penalty would be imposed with regard to an understatement due to a transaction's lack of economic substance in lieu of other accuracy-related penalties that might be levied with respect to the tax understatement, although any understatement arising from a lack of economic substance would be taken into account in determining whether there is a substantial understatement of income tax under current law.

The IRS could assert and abate the new economic substance penalty. The IRS could assert the penalty even if there has not been a court determination that the economic substance doctrine was relevant. Any abatement of the economic substance penalty would have to be proportionate to the abatement of the underlying tax liability.

Denial of Interest Deduction. The proposal would deny any deduction for interest attributable to an understatement of tax arising from the application of the economic substance doctrine.

The proposal would apply to transactions entered into after the date of enactment. The denial of interest deduction component would be effective for taxable years ending after the date of enactment with respect to transactions entered into after such date.

ALLOW ASSESSMENT OF CRIMINAL RESTITUTION AS TAX

Current Law

In criminal tax cases, a District Court may issue an order requiring the defendant to pay restitution of existing tax liabilities. The District Court has authority to order restitution under the criminal provisions of Title 18, not the Internal Revenue Code (Code). Because the assessment procedures under the Code apply only to taxes imposed by the Code, those procedures do not apply to restitution orders issued under Title 18, even if the restitution order relates to an existing tax liability.

Reasons for Change

Because court-ordered restitution in criminal tax cases cannot be assessed as a tax, the IRS cannot use its existing assessment systems to collect and enforce the restitution obligation. This leads to unnecessary duplication of efforts, delays, and confusion in the administration of court-ordered restitution.

Proposal

The proposal would allow the IRS and the Treasury Department to immediately assess, without issuing a statutory notice of deficiency, and collect as a tax debt court-ordered restitution. The taxpayer would not be able to collaterally attack the amount of restitution ordered by the court, but would retain the ability to challenge the method of collection.

The proposal would be effective after December 31, 2011.

REVISE OFFER-IN-COMPROMISE APPLICATION RULES

Current Law

Current law provides that the IRS may compromise any civil or criminal case arising under the internal revenue laws prior to a reference to the Department of Justice for prosecution or defense. In 2006, a new provision was enacted to require taxpayers to make certain nonrefundable payments with any initial offer-in-compromise of a tax case. The new provision requires taxpayers making a lump-sum offer-in-compromise to include a nonrefundable payment of 20 percent of the lump-sum with the initial offer. In the case of an offer-in-compromise involving periodic payments, the initial offer must be accompanied by a nonrefundable payment of the first installment that would be due if the offer were accepted.

Reasons for Change

Requiring nonrefundable payments with an offer-in-compromise may substantially reduce access to the offer-in-compromise program. The offer-in-compromise program is designed to settle cases in which taxpayers have demonstrated an inability to pay the full amount of a tax liability. The program allows the IRS to collect the portion of a tax liability that the taxpayer has the ability to pay. Reducing access to the offer-in-compromise program makes it more difficult and costly to obtain the collectable portion of existing tax liabilities.

Proposal

The proposal would eliminate the requirements that an initial offer-in-compromise include a nonrefundable payment of any portion of the taxpayer's offer.

The proposal would be effective for offers-in-compromise submitted after the date of enactment.

EXPAND IRS ACCESS TO INFORMATION IN THE NATIONAL DIRECTORY OF NEW HIRES FOR TAX ADMINISTRATION PURPOSES

Current Law

The Office of Child Support Enforcement of the Department of Health and Human Services (HHS) maintains the National Directory of New Hires (NDNH), which is a database that contains newly-hired employee data from Form W-4, quarterly wage data from State and Federal employment security agencies, and unemployment benefit data from State unemployment insurance agencies. The NDNH was created to help State child support enforcement agencies enforce obligations of parents across State lines.

Under current provisions of the Social Security Act, the IRS may obtain data from the NDNH, but only for the purpose of administering the Earned Income Tax Credit and verifying employment reported on a tax return.

Generally, the IRS obtains employment and unemployment data less frequently than quarterly, and there are significant internal costs of preparing these data for use. Under various State laws, the IRS may negotiate for access to employment and unemployment data directly from State agencies that maintain these data.

Reasons for Change

Employment data are useful to the IRS in administering a wide range of tax provisions beyond the EITC, including verifying taxpayer claims and identifying levy sources. Currently, the IRS may obtain employment and unemployment data on a State-by-State basis, which is a costly and time-consuming process. NDNH data are timely, uniformly compiled, and electronically accessible. Access to the NDNH would increase the productivity of the IRS by reducing the amount of IRS resources dedicated to obtaining and processing data without reducing the current levels of taxpayer privacy.

Proposal

The Social Security Act would be amended to expand IRS access to NDNH data for general tax administration purposes, including data matching, verification of taxpayer claims during return processing, preparation of substitute returns for non-compliant taxpayers, and identification of levy sources. Data obtained by the IRS from the NDNH would be protected by existing taxpayer privacy law, including civil and criminal sanctions.

The proposal would be effective upon enactment.

MAKE REPEATED WILLFUL FAILURE TO FILE A TAX RETURN A FELONY

Current Law

Current law provides that willful failure to file a tax return is a misdemeanor punishable by a term of imprisonment for not more than one year, a fine of not more than $25,000 ($100,000 in the case of a corporation), or both. A taxpayer who fails to file returns for multiple years commits a separate misdemeanor offense for each year.

Reasons for Change

Increased criminal penalties would help to deter multiple willful failures to file tax returns.

Proposal

Any person who willfully fails to file tax returns in any three years within any five consecutive year period, if the aggregated tax liability for such period is at least $50,000, would be subject to a new aggravated failure to file criminal penalty. The proposal would classify such failure as a felony and, upon conviction, impose a fine of not more than $250,000 ($500,000 in the case of a corporation) or imprisonment for not more than five years, or both.

The proposal would be effective for returns required to be filed after December 31, 2010.

FACILITATE TAX COMPLIANCE WITH LOCAL JURISDICTIONS

Current Law

Although Federal tax returns and return information (FTI) generally are confidential, the IRS and Treasury Department may share FTI with States as well as certain local government entities that are treated as States for this purpose. Generally, the purpose of information sharing is to facilitate tax administration. Where sharing of FTI is authorized, reciprocal provisions generally authorize disclosure of information to the IRS by State and local governments. State and local governments that receive FTI must safeguard it according to prescribed protocols that require secure storage, restricted access, reports to IRS, and shredding or other proper disposal. See, e.g., IRS Publication 1075. Criminal and civil sanctions apply to unauthorized disclosure or inspection of FTI. Indian Tribal Governments (ITGs) are treated as States by the tax law for several purposes, such as certain charitable contributions, excise tax credits, and local tax deductions, but not for purposes of information sharing.

Reasons for Change

IRS and Treasury compliance activity, especially with respect to alcohol, tobacco and fuel excise taxes, may necessitate information sharing with ITGs. For example, the IRS may wish to confirm if a fuel supplier's claim to have delivered particular amounts to adjacent jurisdictions is consistent with that reported to the IRS. If not, the IRS in conjunction with the ITG, which would have responsibility for administering taxes imposed by the ITG, can take steps to ensure compliance with both Federal and ITG tax laws. Where the local government is treated as a State for information sharing purposes, IRS, Treasury, and local officials can support each other's efforts. Where the local government is not so treated, there is an impediment to compliance activity.

Proposal

ITGs that impose alcohol, tobacco, or fuel excise or income or wage taxes would be treated as States for purposes of information sharing to the extent necessary for ITG tax administration. An ITG that receives FTI would be required to safeguard it according to prescribed protocols. The criminal and civil sanctions would apply.

The proposal would be effective for disclosures made after enactment.

EXTEND STATUTE OF LIMITATIONS WHERE STATE ADJUSTMENT AFFECTS FEDERAL TAX LIABILITY

Current Law

In general, additional Federal tax liabilities in the form of tax, interest, penalties and additions to tax must be assessed by the IRS within three years after the date a return is filed. If an assessment is not made within the required time period, the additional liabilities generally cannot be assessed or collected at any future time. The Code contains exceptions to the general statute of limitations. In general, the statute of limitations with respect to claims for refund expires three years from the time the return was filed or two years from the time the tax was paid, whichever is later.

State and local authorities employ a variety of statutes of limitations for State and local tax assessments. Pursuant to agreement, the IRS and State and local revenue agencies exchange reports of adjustments made through examination so that corresponding adjustments can be made by each taxing authority. In addition, States provide the IRS with reports of potential discrepancies between State returns and Federal returns.

Reasons for Change

The general statute of limitations serves as a barrier to the effective use by the IRS of State and local tax adjustment reports when the reports are provided by the State or local revenue agency to the IRS with little time remaining for assessments to be made at the Federal level. Under the current statute of limitations framework, taxpayers may seek to extend the State statute of limitations or postpone agreement to State proposed adjustments until such time as the Federal statute of limitations expires in order to preclude assessment at the Federal level. In addition, it is not always the case that a taxpayer that files an amended State or local return reporting additional liabilities at the State or local level that also affect Federal tax liability will file an amended return at the Federal level.

Proposal

The proposal would create an additional exception to the general three-year statute of limitations for assessment of Federal tax liability resulting from adjustments to State or local tax liability. The statute of limitations would be extended to the greater of: (1) one year from the date the taxpayer first files an amended tax return with the IRS reflecting adjustments to the State or local tax return; or (2) two years from the date the IRS first receives information from the State or local revenue agency under an information sharing agreement in place between the IRS and a State or local revenue agency. The statute of limitations would be extended only with respect to the increase in Federal tax attributable to the State or local tax adjustment. The statute of limitations would not be further extended if the taxpayer files additional amended returns for the same tax periods as the initial amended return or if the IRS receives additional information from the State or local revenue agency under an information sharing agreement. The statute of limitations on claims for refund would be extended correspondingly so that any overall increase in tax assessed by the IRS as a result of the State or local examination report would take into account agreed-upon tax decreases or reductions attributable to a refund or credit.

The proposal would be effective for returns required to be filed after December 31, 2010.

IMPROVE INVESTIGATIVE DISCLOSURE STATUTE

Current Law

Generally, tax return information is confidential, unless a specific exception in the Code applies. In the case of tax administration, the Code permits Treasury and IRS officers and employees to disclose return information to the extent necessary to obtain information not otherwise reasonably available, in the course of an audit or investigation, as prescribed by regulation. Thus, for example, a revenue agent may identify himself or herself as affiliated with the IRS, and may disclose the nature and subject of an investigation, as necessary to elicit information from a witness in connection with that investigation. Criminal and civil sanctions apply to unauthorized disclosures of return information.

Reasons for Change

Treasury Regulations effective since 2003 state that the term "necessary" in this context does not mean essential or indispensable, but rather appropriate and helpful in obtaining the information sought. In other contexts, a "necessary" disclosure is one without which performance cannot be accomplished reasonably without the disclosure. Determining if an investigative disclosure is "necessary" is inherently factual, leading to inconsistent opinions by the courts. Eliminating this uncertainty from the statute would facilitate investigations by IRS officers and employees, while setting forth clear guidance for taxpayers, thus enhancing compliance with the tax Code.

Proposal

The taxpayer privacy law would be clarified by stating that it does not prohibit Treasury and IRS officers and employees from identifying themselves, their organizational affiliation, and the nature and subject of an investigation, when contacting third parties in connection with a civil or criminal tax investigation.

The proposal would be effective for disclosures made after enactment.

Expand Penalties

CLARIFY THAT BAD CHECK PENALTY APPLIES TO ELECTRONIC CHECKS AND OTHER PAYMENT FORMS

Current Law

The Code imposes a penalty on any taxpayer who attempts to satisfy a tax liability with a check or money that is not duly paid. The penalty is 2 percent of the amount of the bad check or money order. If the bad check or money order is for less than $1,250, the penalty is the lesser of $25 or the amount of the check or money order.

Reasons for Change

Taxpayers use a variety of commercially acceptable instruments to pay tax liabilities, but only two types of instruments are covered by the Code's bad check penalty: checks and money orders.

Proposal

The proposal would expand the bad check penalty to cover all commercially acceptable instruments of payment that are not duly paid.

The proposal would be effective for returns required to be filed after December 31, 2010.

IMPOSE A PENALTY ON FAILURE TO COMPLY WITH ELECTRONIC FILING REQUIREMENTS

Current Law

Certain corporations and tax-exempt organizations (including certain charitable trusts and private foundations) are required to file their returns electronically. Generally, filing on paper instead of electronically is treated as a failure to file if electronic filing is required. Additions to tax are imposed for the failure to file tax returns reporting a liability. For failure to file a corporate return, the addition to tax is 5 percent of the amount required to be shown as tax due on the return, for the first month of failure, and an additional 5 percent for each month or part of a month thereafter, up to a maximum of 25 percent.

For failure to file a tax-exempt organization return, the addition to tax is $20 a day for each day the failure continues. The maximum amount per return is $10,000 or 5 percent of the organization's gross receipts for the year, whichever is less. Organizations with annual gross receipts exceeding $1 million, however, are subject to an addition to tax of $100 per day, with a maximum of $50,000.

Reasons for Change

Although there are additions to tax for the failure to file returns, there is no specific penalty for a failure to comply with a requirement to file electronically. Because the addition to tax for failure to file a corporate return is based on an underpayment of tax, no addition is imposed if the corporation is in a refund, credit, or loss status. Thus, the existing addition to tax may not provide an adequate incentive for certain corporations to file electronically. Generally, electronic filing increases efficiency of tax administration because the provision of tax return information in an electronic form enables the IRS to focus audit activities where they can have the greatest impact. This also assists taxpayers where the need for audit is reduced.

Proposal

The proposal would establish an assessable penalty for a failure to comply with a requirement of electronic (or other machine-readable) format for a return that is filed. The amount of the penalty would be $25,000 for a corporation or $5,000 for a tax-exempt organization. For failure to file in any format, the existing penalty would remain, and the proposed penalty would not apply.

The proposal would be effective for returns required to be electronically filed after December 31, 2011.

Modify Estate and Gift Tax Valuation Discounts and Other Reforms

REQUIRE CONSISTENT VALUATION FOR TRANSFER AND INCOME TAX PURPOSES

Current Law [4]

Section 1014 provides that the basis of property acquired from a decedent generally is the fair market value of the property on the decedent's date of death. Similarly, property included in the decedent's gross estate for estate tax purposes generally must be valued at its fair market value on the date of death. Although the same valuation standard applies to both provisions, current law does not explicitly require that the recipient's basis in that property be the same as the value at which that property was reported for estate tax purposes.

Section 1015 provides that the donee's basis in property received by gift during the life of the donor generally is the donor's adjusted basis in the property, increased by gift tax paid on the transfer. If, however, the donor's basis exceeds the fair market value of the property on the date of the gift, the donee's basis is limited to that fair market value for purposes of determining any subsequent loss.

Section 6034A imposes a consistency requirement – specifically, that the recipient of a distribution of income from a trust or estate must report on the recipient's own income tax return the exact information included on the Schedule K-1 of the trust's or estate's income tax return – but this provision applies only for income tax purposes, and the Schedule K-1 does not include basis information.

Reasons for Change

Taxpayers should be required to take consistent positions in dealing with the Internal Revenue Service, whether or not principles of privity apply. If the logic underlying the determination of the new basis in property acquired on the death of the owner is that the new basis is the amount used to determine the decedent's estate tax liability, then the law should require that the same value be used by the recipient, unless that value is in excess of the accurate value. In the case of property transferred on death or by gift during life, often the executor of the estate or the donor, respectively, will be in the best position to ensure that the recipient receives the information that will be necessary to determine the recipient's basis in the transferred property.

Proposal

This proposal would impose both a consistency and a reporting requirement. The basis of property received by reason of death under section 1014 must equal the value of that property for estate tax purposes. The basis of property received by gift during the life of the donor must equal the donor's basis determined under section 1015. This proposal would require that the

---

[4] The Administration's baseline assumes that the laws governing the estate, gift and generation-skipping taxes as in effect during 2009 are extended permanently. Consequently, the discussion of Current Law set forth above reflects the applicable law as in effect during 2009.

basis of the property in the hands of the recipient be no greater than the value of that property as determined for estate or gift tax purposes (subject to subsequent adjustments). A reporting requirement would be imposed on the executor of the decedent's estate and on the donor of a lifetime gift to provide the necessary information to both the recipient and the IRS. A grant of regulatory authority would be included to provide details about the implementation and administration of these requirements, including rules for situations in which no estate tax return is required to be filed or gifts are excluded from gift tax under section 2503, for situations in which the surviving joint tenant or other recipient may have better information than the executor, and for the timing of the required reporting in the event of adjustments to the reported value subsequent to the filing of an estate or gift tax return.

The proposal would be effective as of the date of enactment.

MODIFY RULES ON VALUATION DISCOUNTS

Current Law[5]

The fair market value of property transferred, whether on the death or during the life of the transferor, generally is subject to estate or gift tax at the time of the transfer. Sections 2701 through 2704 of the Internal Revenue Code were enacted to prevent the reduction of taxes through the use of "estate freezes" and other techniques designed to reduce the value of the transferor's taxable estate and discount the value of the taxable transfer to the beneficiaries of the transferor without reducing the economic benefit to the beneficiaries. Generally, section 2704(b) provides that certain "applicable restrictions" (that would normally justify discounts in the value of the interests transferred) are to be ignored in valuing interests in family-controlled entities if those interests are transferred (either by gift or on death) to or for the benefit of other family members. The application of these special rules results in an increase in the transfer tax value of those interests above the price that a hypothetical willing buyer would pay a willing seller, because section 2704(b) generally directs an appraiser to ignore the rights and restrictions that would otherwise support significant discounts for lack of marketability and control.

Reasons for Change

Judicial decisions and the enactment of new statutes in most states, in effect, have made section 2704(b) inapplicable in many situations by recharacterizing restrictions such that they no longer fall within the definition of an "applicable restriction". In addition, the Internal Revenue Service has identified additional arrangements designed to circumvent the application of section 2704.

Proposal

This proposal would create an additional category of restrictions ("disregarded restrictions") that would be ignored in valuing an interest in a family-controlled entity transferred to a member of the family if, after the transfer, the restriction will lapse or may be removed by the transferor and/or the transfer's family. Specifically, the transferred interest would be valued by substituting for the disregarded restrictions certain assumptions to be specified in regulations. Disregarded restrictions would include limitations on a holder's right to liquidate that holder's interest that are more restrictive than a standard to be identified in regulations. A disregarded restriction also would include any limitation on a transferee's ability to be admitted as a full partner or to hold an equity interest in the entity. For purposes of determining whether a restriction may be removed by member(s) of the family after the transfer, certain interests (to be identified in regulations) held by charities or others who are not family members of the transferor would be deemed to be held by the family. Regulatory authority would be granted, including the ability to create safe harbors to permit taxpayers to draft the governing documents of a family-controlled entity so as to avoid the application of section 2704 if certain standards are met. This proposal would make conforming clarifications with regard to the interaction of this proposal with the transfer tax marital and charitable deductions.

---

[5] The Administration's baseline assumes that the laws governing the estate, gift and generation-skipping taxes as in effect during 2009 are extended permanently. Consequently, the discussion of Current Law set forth above reflects the applicable law as in effect during 2009.

This proposal would apply to transfers after the date of enactment of property subject to restrictions created after October 8, 1990 (the effective date of section 2704).

REQUIRE A MINIMUM TERM FOR GRANTOR RETAINED ANNUITY TRUSTS (GRATS)

Current Law

Section 2702 provides that, if an interest in a trust is transferred to a family member, the value of any interest retained by the grantor is valued at zero for purposes of determining the transfer tax value of the gift to the family member(s). This rule does not apply if the retained interest is a "qualified interest." A fixed annuity, such as the annuity interest retained by the grantor of a GRAT, is one form of qualified interest, so the gift of the remainder interest in the GRAT is determined by deducting the present value of the retained annuity during the GRAT term from the fair market value of the property contributed to the trust.

Generally, a GRAT is an irrevocable trust funded with assets expected to appreciate in value, in which the grantor retains an annuity interest for a term of years that the grantor expects to survive. At the end of that term, the assets then remaining in the trust are transferred to (or held in further trust for) the beneficiaries, who generally are descendants of the grantor. If the grantor dies during the GRAT term, however, the trust assets (at least the portion needed to produce the retained annuity) are included in the grantor's gross estate for estate tax purposes. To this extent, although the beneficiaries will own the remaining trust assets, the estate tax benefit of creating the GRAT (specifically, the tax-free transfer of the appreciation during the GRAT term in excess of the annuity payments) is not realized.

Reasons for Change

GRATs have proven to be a popular and efficient technique for transferring wealth while minimizing the gift tax cost of transfers, providing that the grantor survives the GRAT term and the trust assets do not depreciate in value. The greater the appreciation, the greater the transfer tax benefit achieved. Taxpayers have become adept at maximizing the benefit of this technique, often by minimizing the term of the GRAT (thus reducing the risk of the grantor's death during the term), in many cases to two years, and by retaining annuity interests significant enough to reduce the gift tax value of the remainder interest to zero or to a number small enough to generate only a minimal gift tax liability.

Proposal

This proposal would require, in effect, some downside risk in the use of this technique by imposing the requirement that a GRAT have a minimum term of ten years.[6] The proposal would also include a requirement that the remainder interest have a value greater than zero and would prohibit any decrease in the annuity during the GRAT term. Although a minimum term would not prevent "zeroing-out" the gift tax value of the remainder interest, it would increase the risk of the grantor's death during the GRAT term and the resulting loss of any anticipated transfer tax benefit.

This proposal would apply to trusts created after the date of enactment.

---

[6] Cf. section 673 as applicable to a so-called *Clifford* trust created before or on March 1, 1986, with a ten-year minimum term.

UPPER-INCOME TAX PROVISIONS

REINSTATE THE 39.6-PERCENT RATE

Current Law

Prior to the enactment of the Economic Growth Tax Relief Reconciliation Act of 2001 (EGTRRA), the highest individual income tax rate was 39.6 percent. EGTRRA reduced the 39.6-percent tax rate temporarily to 35 percent, with the reduction phased in over several years. The Jobs and Growth Tax Relief Reconciliation Act of 2003 (JGTRRA) accelerated the reduction, and since 2003, the highest statutory individual income tax rate has been 35 percent. For 2010, it applies to taxable income over $373,650. The 35-percent tax rate sunsets after 2010.

Reason for Change

Increasing the income tax liability of higher-income taxpayers would reduce the deficit, make the income tax system more progressive and distribute the cost of government more fairly among taxpayers of various income levels.

Proposal

The Administration's tax receipts baseline assumes a policy of permanently extending the EGTRRA tax rates. This proposal would permit the EGTRRA reduction in the highest income tax rate to sunset after 2010. Thus, beginning in 2011, the highest income tax rate would be 39.6 percent. At 2010 levels, the 39.6-percent rate would apply to taxable incomes over $373,650 for married taxpayers filing jointly, heads of household and single filers. However, the taxable income levels at which this rate begins to apply would be indexed for inflation for 2011 and for each year thereafter.

REINSTATE THE 36-PERCENT RATE FOR TAXPAYERS WITH INCOME OVER $250,000 (MARRIED) AND $200,000 (SINGLE)

Current Law

Prior to the enactment of EGTRRA, the second highest individual income tax rate was 36 percent. EGTRRA reduced the 36-percent tax rate temporarily to 33 percent, with the reduction phased in over several years. JGTRRA accelerated the reduction, and since 2003 the second highest statutory individual income tax rate has been 33 percent. In 2010, it applies to taxable income over $209,250 if married filing jointly ($171,750 if single) but less than the income levels at which the 35-percent rate applies. The 33-percent tax rate sunsets after 2010.

Reason for Change

Increasing the income tax liability of higher-income taxpayers would reduce the deficit, make the income tax system more progressive and distribute the cost of government more fairly among taxpayers of various income levels.

Proposal

The Administration's tax receipts baseline assumes a policy of permanently extending the EGTRRA tax rates. This proposal would permit the EGTRRA reduction in the second highest income tax rate to sunset after 2010. Thus, beginning in 2011, the second highest tax rate would be 36 percent. The taxable income levels at which that rate begins to apply would vary by filing status and would be indexed annually for inflation. The 36-percent tax rate would apply to taxable income above the following amounts but less than the income levels at which the 39.6-percent rate would apply: $250,000 less the standard deduction and two personal exemptions, indexed from 2009, for married taxpayers filing jointly; $200,000 less the standard deduction and one personal exemption, indexed for inflation from 2009, for single filers. The 28-percent tax rate bracket would be expanded so that taxpayers earning less than these amounts would not see their taxes rise as a result of the increased tax rate brackets.

REINSTATE THE LIMITATION ON ITEMIZED DEDUCTIONS FOR TAXPAYERS WITH INCOME OVER $250,000 (MARRIED) AND $200,000 (SINGLE)

Current Law

Individual taxpayers may elect to itemize their deductions instead of claiming a standard deduction. In general, itemized deductions include medical and dental expenses (in excess of 7.5 percent of AGI), state and local property taxes and either income or sales taxes, interest paid, gifts to charities, casualty and theft losses (in excess of 10 percent of AGI), job expenses and certain miscellaneous expenses (some only in excess of 2 percent of AGI).

Prior to the enactment of EGTRRA, otherwise allowable itemized deductions (other than medical expenses, investment interest, theft and casualty losses, and gambling losses) were reduced by 3 percent of the amount by which AGI exceeded a statutory floor that was indexed annually for inflation, but not by more than 80 percent of the otherwise allowable deductions. EGTRRA reduced the itemized deduction limitation in three steps. For 2006 and 2007, itemized deductions were reduced by 2 percent of AGI over the floor, but not by more than 53-1/3 percent. For 2008 and 2009, itemized deductions were reduced by 1 percent of AGI over the floor, but not by more than 26-2/3 percent. For 2010, the reduction was completely eliminated. However, beginning in 2011, the full itemized deduction reduction of 3 percent of AGI exceeding the floor is scheduled to be reinstated.

For 2010, the AGI floor, if it were applicable, would be $167,100 ($83,550 if married filing separately).

Reason for Change

Limiting the tax benefit of higher-income taxpayers' itemized deductions would reduce the deficit, make the income tax system more progressive, and distribute the cost of government more fairly among taxpayers of various income levels.

Proposal

The Administration's tax receipts baseline assumes a policy of permanently extending the EGTRRA repeal of the limitation on itemized deductions. This proposal would allow the elimination of the limitation on itemized deduction enacted in EGTRRA to sunset after 2010. Thus, itemized deductions (other than medical expenses, investment interest, theft and casualty losses, and gambling losses) would be reduced by 3 percent of the amount by which AGI exceeds indexed statutory floors but not by more than 80 percent of the otherwise allowable deductions. For 2011, the AGI floors would be $250,000 for married taxpayers filing jointly and $200,000 for single taxpayers in 2009 dollars, determined as adjusted for inflation between 2009 and 2011. After 2011, the floors would be indexed annually for inflation.

REINSTATE THE PERSONAL EXEMPTION PHASEOUT (PEP) FOR TAXPAYERS WITH INCOME OVER $250,000 (MARRIED) AND $200,000 (SINGLE)

Current Law

Individual taxpayers generally are entitled to a personal exemption for the taxpayer and for each dependent. The amount of each personal exemption is $3,650 for 2010 and is indexed annually for inflation.

Prior to the enactment of EGTRRA, all personal exemptions were reduced or completely phased out simultaneously for higher-income taxpayers. For a taxpayer with adjusted gross income (AGI) in excess of the threshold amount for the taxpayer's filing status, the amount of each personal exemption was reduced by 2 percent of the exemption amount for that year for each $2,500 ($1,250 if married filing separately) or fraction thereof by which AGI exceeded that threshold. EGTRRA reduced the otherwise applicable reduction of personal exemptions by one-third for 2006 and 2007, by two-thirds for 2008 and 2009, and eliminated it completely for 2010. However, beginning in 2011, the full personal exemption phase-out is scheduled to be reinstated.

Reason for Change

Limiting the tax benefit of higher-income taxpayers' personal exemptions would reduce the deficit, make the income tax system more progressive, and distribute the cost of government more fairly among taxpayers of various income levels.

Proposal

The Administration's tax receipts baseline assumes a policy of permanently extending the EGTRRA repeal of the personal exemption phase-out. This proposal would allow the elimination of the personal exemption phase-out enacted in EGTRRA to sunset after 2010. For 2011, the AGI floors would be adjusted for inflation starting with a value of $250,000 in 2009 for married taxpayers filing jointly ($125,000 if filing separately) and $200,000 in 2009 for single taxpayers. After 2011, the AGI floors would be indexed annually for inflation.

IMPOSE A 20-PERCENT RATE ON CAPITAL GAINS AND DIVIDENDS FOR TAXPAYERS WITH INCOME OVER $250,000 (MARRIED) AND $200,000 (SINGLE)

Current Law

A separate rate structure applies to long-term capital gains and qualified dividends. Under current law, the maximum rate of tax on the adjusted net capital gain of an individual is 15 percent. In addition, any adjusted net capital gain otherwise taxed at a 10- or 15-percent rate is taxed at a zero-percent rate. These rates apply for purposes of both the regular tax and the alternative minimum tax (AMT). Qualified dividends generally are taxed at the same rate as capital gains.

Capital losses generally are deductible in full against capital gains. In addition, individual taxpayers may deduct up to $3,000 of capital losses from ordinary income in each year. Any remaining unused capital losses may be carried forward indefinitely to a future year.

The zero- and 15-percent rates for qualified dividends and capital gains are scheduled to sunset for taxable years beginning after December 31, 2010. In 2011, the maximum rate on capital gains would increase to 20 percent, while the tax rates for dividends would go back to the higher ordinary tax rates of up to 39.6 percent.

Reasons for Change

Lower- and middle-income taxpayers should be protected from the tax increase that would otherwise occur in 2011. Allowing the 15-percent rate to expire for high-income taxpayers who are most able to absorb the rate increase would still keep the top rate for long-term capital gains at historically low levels. The 20-percent maximum rate on capital gains would be the same as the maximum capital gains rate enacted in 1987, and is the same as the top rate enacted in 1981. Taxing qualified dividends at the same low rate as capital gains reduces the tax bias against equity investment and helps promote more efficient allocation of capital since investors can choose to reallocate their dividends to the most productive investments.

Proposal

The Administration's tax receipts baseline assumes a policy of permanently extending the zero- and 15-percent tax rates for qualified dividends and long-term capital gains for certain taxpayers. The 0- and 15-percent tax rates for long-term capital gains and qualified dividends would be extended permanently for taxpayers with incomes up to $250,000 for joint returns and $200,000 for single taxpayers. The 20-percent tax rate on long-term capital gains and qualified dividends would apply for married taxpayers filing jointly with income over $250,000 less the standard deduction and two personal exemptions (indexed from 2009) and for single taxpayers with income over $200,000 less the standard deduction and one personal exemption (indexed from 2009). The reduced rates on gains on assets held over 5 years would be repealed.

This proposal is effective for taxable years beginning after December 31, 2010.

LIMIT THE TAX RATE AT WHICH ITEMIZED DEDUCTIONS REDUCE TAX LIABILITY TO 28 PERCENT

Current Law

Current law permits the allowable portion of an individual taxpayer's itemized deductions to reduce the amount of taxable income. This, in effect, applies those deductions first to the taxable income in the highest tax bracket, and then to the next lower tax brackets in descending order.

Individual taxpayers may elect to itemize their deductions instead of claiming a standard deduction. In general, itemized deductions include medical and dental expenses (in excess of 7.5 percent of AGI), state and local property taxes and either income or sales taxes, interest paid, gifts to charities, casualty and theft losses (in excess of 10 percent of AGI), and job expenses and certain miscellaneous expenses (some only in excess of 2 percent of AGI).

For higher-income taxpayers, otherwise allowable itemized deductions (other than medical expenses, investment interest, theft and casualty losses, and gambling losses) were reduced prior to 2010 if AGI exceeds a statutory floor that is indexed annually for inflation. Prior to the enactment of EGTRRA, itemized deductions were reduced by 3 percent of AGI over the threshold but not by more than 80 percent of the otherwise allowable deductions. EGTRRA reduced the itemized deduction limitation in three steps. For 2006 and 2007, itemized deductions were reduced by 2 percent of AGI over the threshold, but not by more than 53-1/3 percent. For 2008 and 2009, itemized deductions were reduced by 1 percent of AGI over the threshold, but not by more than 26-2/3 percent. For 2010, the reduction was completely eliminated. However, beginning in 2011, the full itemized deduction reduction of 3 percent of AGI exceeding the floor, but not by more than 80 percent, is scheduled to be reinstated.

For 2010, the AGI floor, if it were applicable, would be $167,100 ($83,550 if married filing separately).

A separate Budget proposal would adjust the 2011 income thresholds beyond which itemized deductions are reduced to $250,000 (indexed for inflation from 2009) for married taxpayers filing jointly and $200,000 (indexed for inflation from 2009) for single taxpayers. Thereafter, the thresholds would be indexed for inflation annually.

Reasons for Change

Increasing the income tax liability of higher-income taxpayers would reduce the deficit, make the income tax system more progressive, and distribute the cost of government more fairly among taxpayers of various income levels.

Proposal

The proposal would limit the value of all itemized deductions by limiting the tax value of those deductions to 28 percent whenever they would otherwise reduce taxable income in the 36 or 39.6 percent tax brackets. A similar limitation also would apply under the AMT.

This proposal would apply to itemized deductions after they have been reduced under a separate budget proposal that would reinstate the pre-EGTRRA limitation on certain itemized deductions, but with adjusted AGI thresholds in 2011 of $250,000 (indexed from 2009) for married taxpayers filing jointly and $200,000 (indexed from 2009) for other taxpayers. After 2011, these thresholds would be indexed.

The proposal is effective for taxable years beginning after December 31, 2010.

USER FEES

SUPPORT CAPITAL INVESTMENT IN THE INLAND WATERWAYS

Current Law

The Inland Waterways Trust Fund is supported by a 20-cents-per-gallon tax on liquids used as fuel in a vessel in commercial waterway transportation. Commercial waterway transportation is defined as any use of a vessel on any inland or intracoastal waterway of the United States (1) in the business of transporting property for compensation or hire or (2) in transporting property in the business of the owner, lessee, or operator of the vessel (other than fish or other aquatic animal life caught on the voyage). The inland or intracoastal waterways of the United States are the inland and intracoastal waterways of the United States described in section 206 of the Inland Waterways Revenue Act of 1978. Exceptions are provided for deep-draft ocean-going vessels, passenger vessels, State and local governments, and certain ocean-going barges.

Reasons for Change

The fuel excise tax does not raise enough revenue to pay for the users' 50-percent share of the capital costs of the locks and dams that make barge transportation possible on inland and intracoastal waterways. Moreover, the tax is not the most efficient method for financing expenditures on those waterways. Adequate funding for inland and intracoastal waterways can be provided through a more efficient user fee system that is based on lock usage and is tied to the level of spending for inland waterways construction, replacement, expansion, and rehabilitation work.

Proposal

The tax on liquids used as fuel in a vessel in commercial waterway transportation would be phased out and replaced by a fee system based on lock usage. The tax rate would be reduced to 10 cents per gallon beginning January 1, 2013. The tax would be repealed for periods after December 31, 2014. The fee system based on lock usage would be phased in beginning on October 1, 2011. For calendar year 2015 and each subsequent calendar year, the fee schedule would be adjusted as necessary to maintain an appropriate level of net assets in the Inland Waterways Trust Fund.

The proposal would be effective, as described above, upon enactment.

OTHER INITIATIVES

EXTEND AND MODIFY THE NEW MARKETS TAX CREDIT

Current Law

The new markets tax credit (NMTC) is a 39-percent credit for qualified equity investments made to acquire stock in a corporation, or a capital interest in a partnership, that is a qualified community development entity (CDE) that is held for a period of seven years. The allowable credit amount for any given year is the applicable percentage (5 percent for the year the equity interest is purchased from the CDE and for each of the two subsequent years, and 6 percent for each of the following four years) of the amount paid to the CDE for the investment at its original issue. The NMTC is available for a taxable year to the taxpayer who holds the qualified equity investment on the date of the initial investment or on the respective anniversary date that occurs during the taxable year. The credit is recaptured if at any time during the seven-year period that begins on the date of the original issue of the investment the entity ceases to be a qualified CDE, the proceeds of the investment cease to be used as required, or the equity investment is redeemed.

Under current law, the NMTC can be used to offset federal income tax liability but cannot be used to offset alternative minimum tax (AMT) liability.

The NMTC expired on December 31, 2009.

Reasons for Change

A two-year extension of the NMTC would allow CDEs to continue to generate investments in low-income communities.

Proposal

The proposal would extend the new markets tax credit for two years (2010 and 2011), with an allocation amount of $5.0 billion each year, and would make other improvements to the NMTC.

The proposal would be effective upon enactment.

REFORM AND EXTEND BUILD AMERICA BONDS

Current Law

Build America Bonds are a new borrowing tool for State and local governments that were enacted as part of the American Recovery and Reinvestment Act of 2009 ("ARRA"). These bonds are conventional taxable bonds issued by State and local governments. The Treasury Department makes direct payments to State and local governmental issuers (called "refundable tax credits") to subsidize a portion of their borrowing costs in an amount equal to 35 percent of the coupon interest on the bonds. Issuance of Build America Bonds is limited to original financing for public capital projects for which issuers otherwise could use tax-exempt "governmental bonds" (as contrasted with "private activity bonds" which benefit private entities). There are no volume limitations on issuance of Build America Bonds for 2009 and 2010, but authority to issue these bonds expires at the end of 2010. Build America Bonds are an alternative to traditional tax-exempt bonds.

Tax-exempt bonds have broader program parameters than Build America Bonds, and may be used in the following ways: (1) original financing for public capital projects, as with Build America Bonds; (2) "current refundings" to refinance prior governmental bonds for interest cost savings where the prior bonds are repaid promptly within ninety days of issuance of the refunding bonds (as well as one "advance refunding," in which two sets of bonds for the same governmental purpose may remain outstanding concurrently for a period of time longer than ninety days); (3) short-term "working capital" financings for governmental operating expenses for seasonal cash flow deficits (as well as certain longer-term deficit financings which have strict arbitrage restrictions); (4) financing for Code 501(c)(3) nonprofit entities, such as nonprofit hospitals and universities; and (5) qualified private activity bond financing for specified private projects and programs (including, for example, mass commuting facilities, solid waste disposal facilities, low-income residential rental housing projects, and single-family housing for low and moderate income homebuyers), which are subject to annual state bond volume caps with certain exceptions.

Reasons for Change

The Build America Bond program has been successful and has expanded the market for State and local governmental debt. Through December 2009, more than $64 billion in Build America Bonds were issued in over 779 transactions in forty-five States. This program taps into a broader market for investors without regard to tax liability (e.g., pension funds may be investors in Build America Bonds, though they typically do not invest in tax-exempt bonds). This program delivers an efficient Federal subsidy directly to State and local governments (rather than through third-party investors). By comparison, tax-exempt bonds can be viewed as inefficient in that the Federal revenue cost of the tax exemption is often greater than the benefits to State and local governments achieved through lower borrowing costs. This program also has a potentially more streamlined tax compliance framework focusing directly on governmental issuers who benefit from the subsidy, as compared with tax-exempt bonds and tax credit bonds which involve investors as tax intermediaries. This program also has relieved supply pressures in the tax-exempt bond market and has helped to reduce interest rates in that market. Making the Build America Bond program permanent could promote market certainty and greater liquidity.

The present 35-percent Federal subsidy rate for the Build America Bond program represents a deeper Federal borrowing subsidy for temporary stimulus purposes under ARRA than the existing permanent Federal subsidy inherent in tax-exempt bonds. In structuring a permanent Build America Bond program in light of Federal revenue constraints, it is appropriate to develop a revenue neutral Federal subsidy rate relative to the Federal tax expenditure on tax-exempt bonds.

For such a revenue neutral Federal subsidy rate, it also is appropriate to expand the eligible uses for Build America Bonds to include other program purposes for which tax-exempt bonds may be used.

Proposal

Permanent Program for Build America Bonds. This proposal would make the Build America Bonds program permanent at a Federal subsidy level equal to 28 percent of the coupon interest on the bonds. The proposed Federal subsidy level is intended to be approximately revenue neutral relative to the estimated future Federal tax expenditure for tax-exempt bonds. The proposed Federal subsidy rate for Build America Bonds should lessen borrowing costs to State and local governments compared to tax-exempt bonds due to inefficiencies inherent in the tax-exempt bond market.

Expanded Uses. This proposal would also expand the eligible uses for Build America Bonds to include the following: (1) original financing for governmental capital projects, as under the initial authorization of Build America Bonds; (2) current refundings of prior public capital project financings for interest cost savings where the prior bonds are repaid promptly within ninety days of issuance of the current refunding bonds; (3) short-term governmental working capital financings for governmental operating expenses (such as tax and revenue anticipation borrowings for seasonal cash flow deficits), subject to a thirteen-month maturity limitation; and (4) financing for Section 501(c)(3) nonprofit entities, such as nonprofit hospitals and universities.

The proposal would be effective as of January 1, 2011.

RESTRUCTURE ASSISTANCE TO NEW YORK CITY: PROVIDE TAX INCENTIVES FOR TRANSPORATION INFRASTRUCTURE

Current Law

The Job Creation and Worker Assistance Act of 2002 (the Act) provided tax incentives for the area of New York City damaged or affected by the terrorist attacks on September 11, 2001. The Act created the "New York Liberty Zone," defined as the area located on or south of Canal Street, East Broadway (east of its intersection with Canal Street), or Grand Street (east of its intersection with East Broadway) in the Borough of Manhattan in the City of New York, New York. New York Liberty Zone tax incentives included: (1) an expansion of the work opportunity tax credit (WOTC) for New York Liberty Zone business employees; (2) a special depreciation allowance for qualified New York Liberty Zone property; (3) a five-year recovery period for depreciation of qualified New York Liberty Zone leasehold improvement property; (4) $8 billion of tax-exempt private activity bond financing for certain nonresidential real property, residential rental property and public utility property; (5) $9 billion of additional tax-exempt, advance refunding bonds; (6) increased section 179 expensing; and (7) an extension of the replacement period for nonrecognition of gain for certain involuntary conversions.[7]

The expanded WOTC credit provided a 40-percent subsidy on the first $6,000 of annual wages paid to New York Liberty Zone business employees for work performed during 2002 or 2003.

The special depreciation allowance for qualified New York Liberty Zone property equals 30 percent of the adjusted basis of the property for the taxable year in which the property is placed in service. Qualified nonresidential real property and residential rental property must be purchased by the taxpayer after September 10, 2001, and placed in service before January 1, 2010. Such property is qualified property only to the extent it rehabilitates real property damaged, or replaces real property destroyed or condemned, as a result of the September 11, 2001, terrorist attacks.[8]

The five-year recovery period for qualified leasehold improvement property applied, in general, to buildings located in the New York Liberty Zone if the improvement was placed in service after September 10, 2001, and before January 1, 2007, and no written binding contract for the improvement was in effect before September 11, 2001.

The $8 billion of tax-exempt private activity bond financing is authorized to be issued by the State of New York or any political subdivision thereof after March 9, 2002, and before January 1, 2010.

The $9 billion of additional tax-exempt, advance refunding bonds was available after March 9, 2002, and before January 1, 2006, with respect to certain State or local bonds outstanding on September 11, 2001.

---

[7] The Working Families Tax Relief Act of 2004 amended certain of the New York Liberty Zone provisions relating to tax-exempt bonds.

[8] Other qualified property must have been placed in service prior to January 1, 2007.

Businesses were allowed to expense the cost of certain qualified New York Liberty Zone property placed in service prior to 2007, up to an additional $35,000 above the amounts generally available under section 179. In addition, only 50 percent of the cost of such qualified New York Liberty Zone property counted toward the limitation under which section 179 deductions are reduced to the extent the cost of section 179 property exceeds a specified amount.

A taxpayer may elect not to recognize gain with respect to property that is involuntarily converted if the taxpayer acquires within an applicable period (the replacement period) property similar or related in service or use. In general, the replacement period begins with the date of the disposition of the converted property and ends two years (three years if the converted property is real property held for the productive use in a trade or business or for investment) after the close of the first taxable year in which any part of the gain upon conversion is realized. The Act extended the replacement period to five years for property in the New York Liberty Zone that was involuntarily converted as a result of the terrorist attacks on September 11, 2001, if substantially all of the use of the replacement property is in New York City.

Reasons for Change

Some of the tax benefits that were provided to New York following the attacks of September 11, 2001, likely will not be usable in the form in which they were originally provided. State and local officials in New York have concluded that improvements to transportation infrastructure and connectivity in the Liberty Zone would have a greater impact on recovery and continued development than would continuing some of the original tax incentives.

Proposal

The proposal would provide tax credits to New York State and New York City for expenditures relating to the construction or improvement of transportation infrastructure in or connecting to the New York Liberty Zone. New York State and New York City each would be eligible for a tax credit for expenditures relating to the construction or improvement of transportation infrastructure in or connecting to the New York Liberty Zone. The tax credit would be allowed in each year from 2011 to 2020, inclusive, subject to an annual limit of $200 million (for a total of $2 billion in tax credits), and would be divided evenly between the State and the City. Any unused credits below the annual limit would be added to the $200 million annual limit for the following year, including years after 2020. Similarly, expenditures that exceed the annual limit would be carried forward and subtracted from the annual limit in the following year. The credit would be allowed against any payments (other than payments of excise taxes and social security and Medicare payroll taxes) made by the City and State under any provision of the Code, including income tax withholding. The Treasury Department would prescribe such rules as are necessary to ensure that the expenditures are made for the intended purposes. The amount of the credit received would be considered State and local funds for the purpose of any Federal program.

The proposal would be effective on January 1, 2011.

IMPLEMENT UNEMPLOYMENT INSURANCE INTEGRITY LEGISLATION

Current Law

The Federal Unemployment Tax Act (FUTA) currently imposes a Federal payroll tax on employers of 6.2 percent of the first $7,000 paid annually to each employee. Generally, these funds support the administrative costs of the unemployment insurance system. Employers in States that meet certain Federal requirements are allowed a credit against FUTA taxes of up to 5.4 percent, making the minimum net Federal rate 0.8 percent. States also impose an unemployment tax on employers. A State's unemployment insurance taxes are first placed in the State's own clearing account and then deposited into its Federal unemployment insurance trust fund account from which the State pays unemployment benefits. State recoveries of overpayments of unemployment insurance benefits must be similarly deposited and used exclusively to pay unemployment benefits.

While States may assess penalties for overpayments of benefits, amounts collected as penalties or interest on benefit overpayments may be treated as general receipts by the States.

Reasons for Change

States' abilities to reduce benefit overpayments and increase overpayment recoveries are limited by funding. The mandatory redeposit of the collection of all unemployment benefits overpayments prevents States from redirecting some of these amounts to future recovery activity. Although States might use penalties or interest on overpayments to increase collections, there is no requirement that such amounts be directed for additional enforcement activities.

Proposal

The proposal would increase resources for the recovery of State unemployment benefit overpayments and delinquent employer taxes. The proposal would allow States to redirect up to 5 percent of overpayment recoveries to additional enforcement activity. The proposal would require States to impose a penalty of at least 15 percent on recipients of fraudulent overpayments, and penalty revenue would be used exclusively for additional enforcement activity. The proposal would expand the ability to collect benefit overpayments due to a State from income tax refunds owed to a benefit recipient. The proposal would allow States to deposit up to 5 percent of moneys recovered in the course of an unemployment insurance tax investigation into a special fund dedicated to implementing the State Unemployment Tax Act (SUTA) Dumping Prevention Act of 2004 or enforcing State laws relating to employer fraud or tax evasion. The proposal would require employers to report a "start work date" to the National Directory of New Hires for all new hires.

The proposal would be effective upon the date of enactment.

Levy Payments to Federal Contractors with Delinquent Tax Debt

AUTHORIZE POST-LEVY DUE PROCESS

Current Law

Before the IRS can issue a levy for an unpaid federal tax liability, it must give the taxpayer an opportunity for an administrative collection due process (CDP) hearing. As exceptions to this general rule, a CDP hearing is not required prior to the IRS issuing a levy for liabilities that arise from either a state tax refund or a disqualified employment tax levy. A disqualified employment tax levy is any levy served in connection with an employment tax liability if the person subject to the levy or a predecessor requested a CDP hearing with respect to unpaid employment taxes within the two-year period prior to the beginning of the taxable period for which the levy is served. When these exceptions apply, the CDP hearing takes place within a reasonable time after the levy.

Prior to making a disbursement to federal contractors, an automated check for Federal tax liabilities generally occurs using the Federal Payment Levy Program (FPLP). When a tax liability is identified, the IRS issues a CDP notice to the federal contractor, but cannot levy the payment until the CDP requirements are complete.

Reason for Change

When the FPLP identifies a federal contractor as having federal employment tax liabilities, the opportunity to levy payments to the contractor may be lost because the CDP requirements cannot be completed before the payment is made.

Proposal

The proposal would allow the IRS to issue levies prior to a CDP hearing for federal employment tax liabilities of federal contractors identified under the FPLP. When a levy is issued prior to a CDP hearing under this proposal, the taxpayer would have an opportunity for a CDP hearing within a reasonable time after the levy.

The proposal would be effective for levies issued after December 31, 2010.

INCREASE LEVY AUTHORITY TO 100 PERCENT FOR VENDOR PAYMENTS

Current Law

If a federal vendor has an unpaid tax liability, the IRS can levy 100 percent of any payment due to the vendor for goods or services sold or leased to the federal government.

Reason for Change

The statutory language "goods or services sold or leased" has been interpreted as excluding payments for the sale or lease of real estate or other types of property not considered "goods or services."

Proposal

The proposal would clarify that the IRS can levy 100 percent of any payment due to a federal vendor with unpaid tax liabilities, including payments made for the sale or lease of real estate and other types of property not considered "goods or services."

The proposal would be effective for payments made after the date of enactment.

ALLOW OFFSET OF FEDERAL INCOME TAX REFUNDS TO COLLECT DELINQUENT STATE INCOME TAXES FOR OUT-OF-STATE RESIDENTS

Current Law

Generally, the Treasury refunds a taxpayer who makes an overpayment (by withholding or otherwise) of Federal tax. The overpayment amount is reduced by debts of the taxpayer for past-due child support, debts to Federal agencies, fraudulently obtained unemployment compensation, and past-due, legally enforceable State income tax obligations. In the latter case, offset is permitted only if the delinquent taxpayer resides in the State seeking the offset.

Reasons for Change

Under current law, a delinquent taxpayer could escape Federal offset from a State as long as he or she is a non-resident. Foreclosing this possibility would better leverage the capacity of the Federal tax offset program for the country as a whole.

PROPOSAL

Offset of Federal refunds to collect State income tax would be permissible regardless of where the delinquent taxpayer resides.

The proposal would be effective on the date of enactment.

APPENDIX: EXTENDING CURRENT POLICIES

The first step in addressing the nation's fiscal problems is to be forthright about them – and to establish an honest baseline that measures where we are before new policies are enacted. The Administration's Budget does so by adjusting the Budget Enforcement Act (BEA) baseline to reflect the true cost of the current policy path. The BEA baseline, which is commonly used in budgeting and is defined in a now expired statute, with some exceptions reflects the projected receipts level under current law. However, under current law, relief from the AMT expired at the end of 2009, a situation which, if not addressed, would cause millions of Americans to begin paying this additional tax. Furthermore, the 2001 and 2003 tax cuts would expire entirely at the end of 2010. These expirations were written into law not for policy reasons; instead, they reflect decisions made to artificially reduce the cost estimates of AMT relief and the 2001 and 2003 tax cuts in order to fit these policies within certain budget process rules. As a result, the BEA's "current law" baseline is not an accurate reflection of the consequences of continuing with current policies. The Administration's Budget uses an adjusted tax baseline that assumes a policy of continuing AMT relief and the 2001 and 2003 tax cuts, so as to project future receipts under current policy and to better measure the effects of the Administration's proposed policy changes.

Index to inflation the 2009 parameters of the AMT as enacted in the American Recovery and Reinvestment Act of 2009. The Administration's baseline projection of current policy reflects annual indexation of the AMT exemption amounts in effect for taxable year 2009 ($46,700 for single taxpayers, $70,950 for married taxpayers filing a joint return and surviving spouses, and $35,475 for married taxpayers filing a separate return and for estates and trusts); the income thresholds for the 28-percent rate ($87,500 for married taxpayers filing a separate return and $175,000 for all other taxpayers); and the income thresholds for the phaseout of the exemption amounts ($150,000 for married taxpayers filing a joint return and surviving spouses, $112,500 for single taxpayers, and $75,000 for married taxpayers filing a separate return). The baseline projection of current policy also extends AMT relief for nonrefundable personal credits.

Continue the 2001 and 2003 tax cuts. Most of the tax reductions enacted in 2001 and 2003 expire on December 31, 2010. The Administration's baseline projection of current policy continues all of these expiring provisions except for repeal of estate, gift, and generation-skipping transfer (GST) taxes. Estate and gift and GST taxes are assumed to be extended at parameters in effect for calendar year 2009 (a top rate of 45 percent and an exemption amount of $3.5 million).

We also include in the baseline a policy of permanently extending the ARRA's temporary expansion of (a) the refundability of the child tax credit and (b) the earned income tax credit for married couples (which were proposals in the FY 2010 Budget).

TABLES OF REVENUE ESTIMATE

Revenue estimates begin on next page.

Table 1   Revenue Estimates of FY 2011 Budget Proposals 1/ 2/ 3/

						Fiscal Years							
	2010	2011	2012	2013	2014	2015	2016	2017	2018	2019	2020	2011-2015	2011-2020
						(in millions of dollars)							
Temporary recovery measures													
Extend the making work pay tax credit 4/	0	-30,132	-31,075	0	0	0	0	0	0	0	0	-61,207	-61,207
Provide $250 refundable credit for Federal, State and local government retirees not eligible for social security benefits 4/	-38	-212	0	0	0	0	0	0	0	0	0	-212	-212
Extend COBRA health insurance premium assistance 4/	-3,188	-5,237	-228	0	0	0	0	0	0	0	0	-5,465	-5,465
Provide additional tax credits for investment in qualified property used in a qualified advanced energy manufacturing project	0	-284	-731	-1,145	-1,114	-539	-122	72	114	62	26	-3,813	-3,661
Extend temporary increase in expensing for small businesses	-706	-440	434	268	186	135	76	43	24	15	12	583	753
Extend temporary bonus depreciation for certain property	-22,445	-15,216	11,912	7,478	5,149	3,912	2,580	1,685	1,063	792	744	13,235	20,099
Extend option for cash assistance to States in lieu of housing tax credits 4/	-2,435	-1,798	91	269	429	511	538	538	538	538	538	-498	2,192
Subtotal, temporary recovery measures	-28,812	-53,319	-19,597	6,870	4,660	4,019	3,072	2,338	1,739	1,407	1,320	-57,377	-47,501
Tax cuts for families and individuals													
Expand the earned income tax credit (EITC) 4/	0	-85	-1,674	-1,645	-1,636	-1,628	-1,639	-1,663	-1,692	-1,730	-1,766	-6,668	-15,158
Expand the child and dependent care tax credit 4/	0	-377	-1,345	-1,359	-1,368	-1,373	-1,377	-1,374	-1,365	-1,354	-1,349	-5,822	-12,641
Provide for automatic enrollment in IRAs and double the tax credit for small employer plan startup costs 4/	0	0	-506	-825	-876	-982	-1,113	-1,261	-1,423	-1,604	-1,801	-3,189	-10,391
Expand saver's credit 4/	0	-323	-2,683	-2,996	-3,029	-3,109	-3,195	-3,323	-3,490	-3,716	-3,910	-12,140	-29,774
Extend American opportunity tax credit 4/	0	-951	-6,875	-7,444	-7,815	-8,400	-8,841	-8,632	-8,738	-8,870	-8,907	-31,485	-75,473
Subtotal, tax cuts for families and individuals	0	-1,736	-13,083	-14,269	-14,724	-15,492	-16,165	-16,253	-16,708	-17,274	-17,733	-59,304	-143,437
Tax cuts for businesses													
Eliminate capital gains taxation on investments in small business stock	-3,044	-5,346	-5,969	-6,622	-55	-280	-731	-1,217	-1,591	-1,933	-2,248	-335	-8,055
Make research & experimentation tax credit permanent	0	0	0	0	-7,286	-7,945	-8,597	-9,244	-9,887	-10,530	-11,182	-33,168	-82,608
Remove cell phones from listed property	-69	-277	-226	-238	-248	-266	-281	-296	-314	-332	-348	-1,255	-2,826
Subtotal, tax cuts for businesses	-3,113	-5,623	-6,195	-6,860	-7,589	-8,491	-9,609	-10,757	-11,792	-12,795	-13,778	-34,758	-93,489
Continue certain expiring provisions through calendar year 2011 4/	-8,867	-21,539	-11,926	-2,205	-1,581	-1,422	-1,309	-1,013	-1,138	-1,435	-3,109	-38,673	-46,677
Other revenue changes and loophole closers													
Reform treatment of financial institutions and products:													
Impose a financial crisis responsibility fee	0	8,000	8,000	9,000	9,000	9,000	9,000	9,000	9,000	10,000	10,000	43,000	90,000
Require accrual of income on forward sale of corporate stock	1	5	12	19	26	33	36	38	40	42	44	95	295
Require ordinary treatment of income from day-to-day dealer activities for certain dealers of equity options and commodities	49	169	214	226	240	254	270	286	303	321	341	1,103	2,624
Modify the definition of "control" for purposes of section 249	2	15	30	32	34	36	38	41	43	46	48	147	363
subtotal, reform treatment of financial institutions and products	52	8,189	8,256	9,277	9,300	9,323	9,344	9,365	9,386	10,409	10,433	44,345	93,282
Reinstate Superfund taxes													
Reinstate Superfund excise taxes	0	440	611	650	689	724	756	787	808	833	857	3,114	7,155
Reinstate Superfund environmental income tax	0	763	997	1,079	1,148	1,197	1,239	1,281	1,321	1,363	1,382	5,184	11,770
subtotal, reinstate Superfund taxes	0	1,203	1,608	1,729	1,837	1,921	1,995	2,068	2,129	2,196	2,239	8,298	18,925
Make unemployment insurance surtax permanent	0	0	1458	1501	1539	1571	1596	1616	1631	1642	1642	6,069	14,196
Repeal LIFO method of accounting for inventories	0	0	2,667	6,007	7,070	7,120	7,162	7,224	7,207	7,278	7,350	22,884	59,085
Repeal gain limitation for dividends received in reorganization exchanges	0	46	77	78	78	81	83	85	86	86	88	360	788
Reform U.S. international tax system:													
Defer deduction of interest expense related to deferred income	0	2,024	3,357	3,343	3,350	3,434	3,520	3,572	3,803	613	626	15,508	25,642
Foreign tax credit reform: Determine the foreign tax credit on a pooling basis	0	1,928	3,198	3,184	3,191	3,271	3,353	3,403	3,439	3,462	3,532	14,772	31,961
Foreign tax credit reform: Prevent splitting of foreign income and foreign taxes	0	1,226	2,223	2,494	2,707	2,875	3,006	3,106	3,186	3,253	3,327	11,525	27,403
Tax currently excess returns associated with transfers of intangibles offshore	0	635	1,580	1,573	1,577	1,616	1,657	1,681	1,699	1,711	1,745	6,981	15,474
Limit shifting of income through intangible property transfers	0	12	32	54	78	104	131	159	189	220	254	280	1,233
Disallow the deduction for excess non-taxed reinsurance premiums paid to affiliates	0	22	53	54	54	50	50	54	58	60	64	233	519
Limit earnings stripping by expatriated entities	0	211	352	353	356	368	379	385	390	393	402	1,640	3,589
Repeal 80/20 company rules	0	83	111	111	112	116	120	122	123	124	127	533	1,149
Prevent the avoidance of dividend withholding taxes	219	275	135	91	94	96	97	102	109	115	123	691	1,237
Modify the tax rules for dual capacity taxpayers	0	381	676	734	788	846	907	972	1,044	1,121	1,080	3,425	8,549
Combat under-reporting of income through use of accounts and entities in offshore jurisdictions	27	72	161	716	919	447	381	549	686	740	762	2,315	5,433
subtotal, reform U.S. international tax system	246	6,869	11,878	12,707	13,226	13,223	13,601	14,105	12,726	11,812	12,042	57,903	122,189
Reform treatment of insurance companies and products:													
Modify rules that apply to sales of life insurance contracts	0	22	71	84	101	117	136	156	179	204	233	395	1,303
Modify dividends-received deduction for life insurance company separate accounts	0	149	379	407	432	441	468	492	511	512	515	1,808	4,306
Expand pro rata interest expense disallowance for corporate-owned life insurance (COLI)	0	20	87	183	276	437	659	910	1,293	1,731	2,188	1,003	7,784

Fiscal Years

(in millions of dollars)

Provision	2010	2011	2012	2013	2014	2015	2016	2017	2018	2019	2020	2011-2015	2011-2020
Permit partial annuitization of a nonqualified annuity contract	0	5	21	39	59	81	105	132	160	192	226	205	1,020
subtotal, reform treatment of insurance companies and products	0	196	558	713	868	1,076	1,368	1,690	2,143	2,639	3,162	3,411	14,413
Eliminate fossil fuel preferences:													
Eliminate oil and gas preferences:													
Repeal enhanced oil recovery credit 5/	0	0	0	0	0	0	0	0	0	0	0	0	0
Repeal credit for oil and gas produced from marginal wells 5/	0	0	0	0	0	0	0	0	0	0	0	0	0
Repeal expensing of intangible drilling costs	0	1,202	1,582	1,089	914	848	694	482	374	344	310	5,635	7,839
Repeal deduction for tertiary injectants	0	5	9	9	8	7	6	6	5	6	6	38	67
Repeal exemption to passive loss limitation for working interests in oil and natural gas properties	0	20	24	19	18	17	17	17	16	16	16	98	180
Repeal percentage depletion for oil and natural gas wells	0	522	895	933	969	1,009	1,052	1,095	1,141	1,184	1,226	4,328	10,026
Repeal domestic manufacturing deduction for oil and gas production	0	851	1,470	1,559	1,650	1,742	1,831	1,920	2,007	2,096	2,188	7,272	17,314
Increase geological and geophysical amortization period for independent producers to seven years	0	44	160	246	231	177	122	67	28	17	18	858	1,110
subtotal, eliminate oil and gas preferences	0	2,644	4,140	3,855	3,790	3,800	3,722	3,587	3,571	3,663	3,764	18,229	36,536
Eliminate coal preferences:													
Repeal expensing of exploration and development costs	0	32	55	49	45	45	44	40	37	34	32	226	413
Repeal percentage depletion for hard mineral fossil fuels	0	57	98	102	106	109	111	115	119	122	123	472	1,062
Repeal capital gains treatment for royalties	10	18	25	48	67	78	87	95	103	111	119	236	751
Repeal domestic manufacturing deduction for coal and other hard mineral fossil fuels	0	3	5	5	5	6	6	6	7	7	7	24	57
subtotal, eliminate coal preferences	10	110	183	204	223	238	248	256	266	274	281	958	2,283
Tax carried (profit) interests as ordinary income	10	2,754	4,323	4,059	4,013	4,038	3,970	3,843	3,837	3,937	4,045	19,187	38,819
Modify the cellulosic biofuel producer credit	0	1,452	3,289	3,914	3,741	3,176	2,534	1,975	1,530	1,355	1,011	15,572	23,977
Eliminate the advanced earned income tax credit 4/	784	6,569	8,058	4,901	2,659	1,491	309	0	0	0	0	23,678	23,987
Deny deduction for punitive damages	0	120	72	70	69	68	69	69	72	74	77	399	760
(provision — label not legible)	0	0	22	32	33	34	35	36	38	38	39	121	307
Repeal lower-of-cost-or-market inventory accounting method	0	0	286	1,423	2,045	1,402	1,127	283	296	309	323	5,156	7,494
Reduce the tax gap and make reforms:													
Expand Information Reporting:													
Require information reporting on payments to corporations	0	84	612	777	924	983	1,040	1,095	1,152	1,212	1,275	3,380	9,154
Require information reporting for rental property expense payments	0	179	267	281	296	312	327	342	357	372	387	1,335	3,120
Require information reporting for private separate accounts of life insurance companies	0	1	2	3	4	4	6	7	8	10	13	14	58
Require a certified Taxpayer Identification Number from contractors and allow certain withholding	0	17	44	63	72	76	79	83	86	90	94	272	704
Require increased information reporting for certain government payments for property and services	0	25	70	58	28	30	32	34	35	37	39	211	388
Increase information return penalties	0	20	34	35	35	36	42	43	43	44	44	160	376
subtotal, expand information reporting	0	326	1,029	1,217	1,359	1,441	1,526	1,604	1,681	1,765	1,852	5,372	13,800
Improve compliance by businesses:													
Require greater electronic filing of returns					No Revenue Effect								
Implement standards clarifying when employee leasing companies can be held liable for their clients' Federal employment taxes	0	11	214	543	688	766	848	933	1,020	1,112	1,208	2,222	7,343
Increase certainty with respect to worker classification	0	4	6	6	7	7	7	8	8	9	9	30	71
subtotal, improve compliance by businesses	0	15	220	549	695	773	855	941	1,028	1,121	1,217	2,252	7,414
Strengthen tax administration:													
Codify "economic substance" doctrine	0	23	77	157	272	366	476	593	682	758	838	895	4,242
Allow assessment of criminal restitution as tax	0	0	3	4	4	4	4	4	4	4	4	15	35
Revise offer-in-compromise application rules	1	3	3	3	3	3	3	3	3	3	4	15	31
Expand IRS access to information in the National Directory of New Hires for tax administration purposes					No Revenue Effect								
Make repeated willful failure to file a tax return a felony	0	0	0	0	1	1	1	1	2	2	2	2	10
Facilitate tax compliance with local jurisdictions	0	0	0	0	0	1	1	1	1	1	1	1	6
Extension of statute of limitations where State adjustment affects Federal tax liability	0	3	4	4	4	4	5	5	5	5	6	19	45
Improve investigative disclosure statute	0	0	0	1	1	2	1	1	2	2	2	4	10
subtotal, strengthen tax administration	1	29	87	168	285	380	491	608	699	775	857	949	4,379
Expand penalties:													
Clarify that bad check penalty applies to electronic checks and other payment forms	0	1	2	2	2	3	3	3	3	4	4	10	27
Impose a penalty on failure to comply with electronic filing requirements	0	0	0	0	0	1	1	1	2	2	2	1	9
subtotal, expand penalties	1	1	2	2	2	4	4	4	5	6	6	11	36
subtotal, reduce the tax gap and make reforms	1	371	1,338	1,936	2,341	2,598	2,876	3,157	3,413	3,667	3,932	8,584	25,629
Modify estate and gift valuation discounts and other reforms:													
Require consistent valuation for transfer and income tax purposes	40	135	171	182	192	204	216	229	243	258	273	884	2,103
Modify rules on valuation discounts	0	666	1,413	1,531	1,671	1,818	1,972	2,135	2,305	2,484	2,672	7,099	18,667
Require a minimum term for grantor retained annuity trusts (GRATs)	0	15	46	93	160	231	308	389	477	570	670	545	2,959

	2010	2011	2012	2013	2014	2015	2016	2017	2018	2019	2020	2011-2015	2011-2020
								Fiscal Years					
								(in millions of dollars)					
subtotal, estate and gift	*40*	*816*	*1,630*	*1,806*	*2,023*	*2,253*	*2,496*	*2,753*	*3,025*	*3,312*	*3,615*	*8,528*	*23,729*
Subtotal, other revenue changes and loophole closers	**1,133**	**28,585**	**45,520**	**50,153**	**50,842**	**49,375**	**48,565**	**48,269**	**47,519**	**48,754**	**49,998**	**224,475**	**467,580**
Upper-income tax provisions													
Reinstate the 39.6% rate	0	12,829	23,625	26,379	29,292	32,074	34,871	37,682	40,527	43,467	46,622	124,199	327,368
Reinstate the 36% rate for taxpayers with income over $250,000 (married) and $200,000 (single)	0	1,680	2,592	2,916	3,264	3,602	3,938	4,278	4,608	4,932	5,261	14,054	37,071
Reinstate the limitation on itemized deductions (Pease) for taxpayers with income over $250,000 (married) and $200,000 (single)	0	5,159	11,230	12,834	14,221	15,564	16,857	18,127	19,340	20,472	21,518	59,008	155,322
Reinstate the personal exemption phaseout (PEP) for taxpayers with income over $250,000 (married) and $200,000 (single)	0	1,681	3,695	4,285	4,770	5,244	5,714	6,197	6,714	7,215	7,652	19,675	53,167
Impose 20% rate on capital gains and dividends for taxpayers with income over $250,000 (married) and $200,000 (single)	1,344	12,165	-263	3,315	8,230	11,372	12,370	13,288	14,162	14,973	15,752	34,819	105,364
Limit the tax rate at which itemized deductions reduce tax liability to 28%	0	7,896	21,582	24,500	27,019	29,351	31,570	33,938	36,268	38,426	40,625	110,348	291,175
Subtotal, upper-income tax provisions	**1,344**	**41,410**	**62,461**	**74,229**	**86,796**	**97,207**	**105,320**	**113,510**	**121,619**	**129,485**	**137,430**	**362,103**	**969,467**
User fees													
Support capital investment in the inland waterways	0	0	196	163	187	129	100	72	70	68	68	675	1,053
Other initiatives													
Extend and modify the new markets tax credit	0	-113	-229	-345	-430	-480	-511	-510	-441	-279	-103	-1,597	-3,441
Reform and extend build America bonds 4/	0	8	-3	-3	-3	-4	-4	-4	-4	-4	-3	-5	-24
Restructure assistance to New York City Provide tax incentives for transportation infrastructure	0	-200	-200	-200	-200	-200	-200	-200	-200	-200	-200	-1,000	-2,000
Implement unemployment insurance integrity legislation	0	0	42	42	16	-4	-75	-175	189	-138	-179	96	-282
Levy payments to Federal contractors with delinquent tax debt:													
Authorize post-levy due process	0	77	115	119	124	109	113	118	122	127	132	544	1,156
Increase levy authority to 100% for vendor payments	0	61	87	36	90	78	82	85	88	92	96	402	845
subtotal, levy payments to Federal contractors with delinquent tax debt	0	138	202	205	214	187	195	203	210	219	228	946	2,001
Allow offset of Federal income tax refunds to collect delinquent State income taxes for out-of-state residents					*No Revenue Effect*								
Subtotal, other initiatives	**0**	**-167**	**-188**	**-301**	**-403**	**-501**	**-595**	**-686**	**-246**	**-402**	**-257**	**-1,560**	**-3,746**
Total Effect of FY 2011 Budget Tax Proposals Relative to Current Policy	**-38,315**	**-12,389**	**57,188**	**107,780**	**118,178**	**124,824**	**129,379**	**135,480**	**141,063**	**147,808**	**153,939**	**395,581**	**1,103,250**

Department of the Treasury

Notes:

1/ Presentation in this table does not reflect the order in which these proposals were estimated.

2/ Appendix A details the budgetary impact of extending certain tax policies relative to current law. These extensions are estimates before the other policy proposals that follow in this table.

3/ Table 14-3 in the Analytical Perspectives of the FY 2011 Budget includes the effects of a number of proposals that are not reflected here. These proposals include the interaction of the $250 economic recovery payments with the making work pay tax credit, increase fees for Migratory Bird Hunting and Conservation Stamps, change retention policy for consular fees, trade initiatives, implement program integrity allocation adjustments – IRS, revise terrorism risk insurance program and the allowances for health insurance reform and jobs initiatives.

4/ This provision affects both receipts and outlays. The combined effects are shown here and the outlays effects included in these estimates are detailed in Appendix B.

5/ This provision is estimated to zero receipt effect under the Administration's current projections for energy prices.

152

Appendix A: Bridge from the Budget Enforcement Act Baseline to Current Policy Baseline 1/

						Fiscal Years							
	2010	2011	2012	2013	2014	2015	2016	2017	2018	2019	2020	2011-2015	2011-2020
						(in millions of dollars)							
Adjustments to reflect current policy:													
Index to inflation the 2009 parameters of the alternative minimum tax as enacted in the American Recovery and Reinvestment Act	-12,957	-64,062	-32,378	-37,907	-45,102	-53,220	-62,494	-72,492	-84,034	-96,809	-110,263	-232,669	-658,761
Continue the 2001 and 2003 tax cuts:													
Permanently extend the 2009 estate tax law	-2,034	6,176	-18,858	-23,701	-26,005	-28,052	-30,215	-32,168	-34,255	-36,519	-38,841	-90,440	-262,438
Tax dividends with a 0%/15% rate structure	-2,263	-22,869	-4,070	-12,415	-21,501	-26,648	-27,634	-28,619	-29,378	-29,884	-30,236	-87,503	-233,254
Tax capital gains with a 0%/15% rate structure	-854	-7,737	-1,535	-4,883	-9,429	-12,275	-13,288	-14,211	-15,107	-15,959	-16,772	-35,859	-111,196
Expand expensing for small businesses		-3,174	-5,608	-4,352	-3,482	-2,838	-2,345	-2,035	-1,868	-1,784	-1,753	-19,454	-29,239
Marginal individual income tax rate reductions		-80,985	-124,474	-135,234	-145,800	-155,995	-166,159	-176,260	-186,268	-196,332	-206,691	-642,488	-1,574,198
Repeal the limitation on itemized deductions (Pease)		-4,576	-9,702	-10,832	-12,010	-13,144	-14,238	-15,318	-16,340	-17,297	-18,193	-50,264	-131,650
Repeal the personal exemption phaseout (PEP)		-1,591	-3,377	-3,809	-4,259	-4,698	-5,131	-5,587	-6,076	-6,553	-6,984	-17,734	-48,065
Increase the child credit 2/		-3,994	-28,144	-28,201	-28,358	-28,481	-28,626	-28,737	-28,843	-28,934	-28,990	-117,178	-261,308
Provide marriage penalty relief 2/		-15,030	-27,580	-29,169	-30,945	-32,741	-34,288	-35,916	-37,574	-39,051	-40,431	-135,465	-322,725
Provide education incentives		-735	-1,367	-1,435	-1,505	-1,578	-1,653	-1,731	-1,813	-1,895	-1,981	-6,620	-15,693
Provide other incentives for families and children	3	-420	-894	-911	-924	-942	-959	-978	-993	-1,008	-1,025	-4,091	-9,054
Expand earned income tax credit by providing marriage penalty relief 2/	5	-21	-1,740	-1,687	-1,659	-1,627	-1,617	-1,612	-1,618	-1,631	-1,654	-6,734	-14,866
Reduce the earnings threshold for the refundable portion of the child tax credit to $3,000 2/	0	0	-9,579	-9,414	-9,341	-9,198	-9,156	-9,068	-9,096	-9,120	-9,148	-27,532	-83,120
Total Effect of Adjustments to BEA Baseline to reflect Current Policy	**-18,100**	**-199,018**	**-269,306**	**-303,950**	**-340,320**	**-371,437**	**-397,803**	**-424,732**	**-453,263**	**-482,776**	**-512,962**	**-1,484,031**	**-3,755,567**

Department of the Treasury

Notes:
1/ Proposals in this table are estimated before the proposals in Table 1.
2/ This provision affects both receipts and outlays. The combined effects are shown here and the outlays effects included in these estimates are detailed in Appendix B.

Appendix B: Outlay Effects Included in Revenue Estimates

						Fiscal Years							
	2010	2011	2012	2013	2014	2015	2016	2017	2018	2019	2020	2011-2015	2011-2020
						(in millions of dollars)							
Increase the child credit	0	759	15,179	15,133	15,122	14,965	14,894	14,829	14,859	14,925	14,983	61,158	135,648
Provide marriage penalty relief	0	-583	2,411	2,307	2,239	2,165	2,111	2,085	2,068	2,079	2,117	8,539	18,999
Expand earned income tax credit by providing marriage penalty relief	0	0	1,656	1,606	1,580	1,547	1,539	1,535	1,542	1,555	1,576	6,389	14,136
Reduce the earnings threshold for the refundable portion of the child tax credit to $3,000	0	0	9,579	9,414	9,341	9,198	9,156	9,068	9,096	9,120	9,148	37,532	83,120
Extend the making work pay tax credit	0	703	21,265	0	0	0	0	0	0	0	0	21,968	21,968
Provide $250 refundable credit for federal, state and local government retirees not eligible for social security benefits	0	100	0	0	0	0	0	0	0	0	0	100	100
Extend COBRA health insurance premium assistance	319	524	23	0	0	0	0	0	0	0	0	547	547
Extend option for cash assistance to States in lieu of housing tax credits	2,435	1,815	0	0	0	0	0	0	0	0	0	1,815	1,815
Expand the earned income tax credit (EITC)	0	83	1,667	1,635	1,628	1,622	1,634	1,659	1,689	1,726	1,762	6,635	15,105
Expand the child and dependent care tax credit	0	0	399	406	403	398	403	406	408	407	409	1,606	3,639
Provide for automatic enrollment in IRAs and double the tax credit for small employer plan startup costs	0	0	83	146	149	158	177	200	223	250	281	536	1,667
Expand savers credit	0	570	3,715	1,402	1,369	1,366	1,349	1,337	1,339	1,340	1,353	8,422	15,140
Extend American opportunity tax credit	0	0	2,941	3,058	3,146	3,268	3,441	3,363	3,330	3,310	3,302	12,413	29,159
Continue certain expiring provisions through calendar year 2011	66	91	23									114	114
Eliminate the advanced earned income tax credit	0	-120	-72	-70	-69	-68	-69	-69	-72	-74	-77	-399	-760
Reform and extend build America bonds	0	266	1,216	2,630	4,108	5,608	7,105	8,595	10,078	11,554	13,023	13,828	64,183
Total Outlay Effect of Proposals	**2,820**	**4,208**	**60,085**	**37,667**	**39,016**	**40,227**	**41,740**	**43,008**	**44,560**	**46,192**	**47,877**	**181,203**	**404,580**

Department of the Treasury

www.ingramcontent.com/pod-product-compliance
Lightning Source LLC
Chambersburg PA
CBHW080251180526
45167CB00006B/2488